Everyone a Leader

A Grassroots Model for the New Workplace

Horst Bergmann
Kathleen Hurson
Darlene Russ-Eft

John Wiley & Sons, Inc.

New York • Chichester • Weinheim • Brisbane • Singapore • Toronto

Published by John Wiley & Sons, Inc.
Published simultaneously in Canada.

This publication is designed to provide accurate and authoritative information in regard to the subject matter covered. It is sold with the understanding that the publisher is not engaged in rendering professional services. If legal, accounting, medical, psychological or any other expert assistance is required, the services of a competent professional person should be sought.

Library of Congress Cataloging-in-Publication Data:
Bergmann, Horst.
    Everyone a leader: a grassroots model for the new workplace /
Horst Bergmann, Kathleen Hurson, Darlene Russ-Eft.
        p.   cm.
    Includes bibliographical references (p.   ) and index.
    ISBN 0-471-19763-7 (cloth: alk. paper)
    1. Leadership.   2. Management.   3. Supervision of employees.
4. Customer relations.   I. Russ-Eft, Darlene F.   II. Hurson,
Kathleen.   III. Title.
HD57.7.B47   1999
658.4'092—dc21   98-49084
                                        CIP

Printed in the United States of America.

10 9 8 7 6 5 4 3 2 1

To our clients, colleagues, and friends who strive to live as grassroots leaders.

CONTENTS

ACKNOWLEDGMENTS

First and foremost, we want to thank Barry Schwenkmeyer for his enormous contribution to this book. With the help of his extraordinary intelligence and remarkable insights, we were able to bring to life what could have been dry research findings. We feel blessed to have him as part of our team.

Many of our associates at AchieveGlobal provided us with invaluable support. Amy Avergun deserves special recognition for her thorough review, critical commentary, and insightful comments on each page of this book.

The research efforts were accomplished through the capable hands of Lilanthi Ravishankar, Judith Richterman, and Julie Winkle.

We are also very grateful for the review and feedback on the materials provided by Todd Warren Beck, Constance Bentley, Jennifer Berkley, Caryl Berrey, Joseph Boschi, Karen Brennan, Camille M. Busette, Martha L. Chamberlain, Darlene Coker, Marcia Corbett, Ed Del Gaizo, Audrey Ellison, Randie Guest, Juan F. Gutierrez, Howard Kamens, Maureen Kelly,

Alexandra Lang, John LaVeck, J. J. Martin, John Mulholland, Craig Perrin, Lynn Piecuch, Cornelien Posada, Susan Muttart, Bill Silberman, and Joyce Thompsen. Nan Lyon, Roz Madden, and Michelle Soto provided stellar administrative support.

The research efforts received assistance or critical review by the researchers at the American Institutes for Research: Kristi Andes, Donald McLaughlin, Jeanne Moulton, and Roger Levine.

Our international colleagues were invaluable in helping us to gain entry to organizations in their respective countries: Colin Duncan of AchieveGlobal UK, Pat Sheridan of Achieve-Global Ireland Training & Development Ltd., and Rod Smart of AchieveGlobal Australia.

We received additional critical commentary from our colleagues in other Times Mirror Companies: Jeanne Hartley of the *Los Angeles Times,* and Durrie Monsma and William C. Lockwood of Jeppesen Sanderson.

We also want to thank John Harrison and Jan Stiles for helping us with early drafts of the book, and Margaret McGuan and Lilia Schwartz for helping with needed administrative support.

Most of all, we are indebted to the numerous unnamed people who contributed their insights on leadership through the critical incidents. We can, however, recognize the following individuals who agreed to participate in lengthy telephone or in-person interviews: Major Greg Balzer, U.S. Marine Corps Recruiting Command; Michelle Bauman, United Express, Atlantic Coast Airlines; Des Byrne, Wavin Ireland, Ltd.; Jerry Carr, Rochester Telephone; Janet H. Clement, Office of Management Excellence, U.S. Mint; Lorraine Cosgrove, Intel Ireland Ltd.; Jack Crouch, Prime Tanning; Peter Dean, The Wharton School and The University of Tennessee; John Eft, Office of Counsel, U.S. Army Corps of Engineers; Steven B. Falk, San Francisco Newspaper Agency; Kenneth Farrell, The Farrell Group; Monica Gleeson, Sigma Wireless Communications; Judy Goetz, Fidelity and Deposit Company of Maryland; Jordan Goldstein, Gensler Architecture Design Planning Worldwide; Merry Goodenough, Office of Counsel, U.S. Army Corps of Engineers; Colm Gorman, Intel Ireland Ltd.; Jeremy Hay, Cendant PHH; Greg Hense, EPCOR Utilities Inc.; Jo Dee Hughes, Honeywell Avionics; Tina Kannapel, U.S. Marshals Service; Gary J. Kral, Cessna

Aircraft Company; Max Lil, Industrial Incineration; Mary Lucas, Cort Furniture Rental; Christopher Lydon, consultant; Judy McTighe, U.S. Census Bureau; Gil Murdoch, Lafarge Construction Materials; Anthony O'Dowd, COREL Corporation Ltd.; Timothy Olson, U.S. Census Bureau; Lieutenant Colonel Jack Pharris, U.S. Marine Corps Recruiting Command; Angie Risley, Whitbread PLC; Colonel Clyde Slick, U.S. Marine Corps; Rex Smitherman, Department of Commerce; Olga Vives, BT Office Products International; Robert Wasley, Raychem Corporation.

FOREWORD

Leadership Counts

COMPETITIVE EXCELLENCE REQUIRES STRONG LEADERSHIP. PEOPLE IN organizations need and respond to leadership. Yet often, leadership seems in short supply. This book aims to help.

Leaders need to create exciting visions of a better future, which are then made concrete through ambitious and measurable goals that galvanize people and get them moving in the same direction. Far too few individuals within organizations know how to do this. Fewer still are prepared for the daily, grassroots give-and-take required of anyone who is serious about turning visions and goals into results. These are challenges men and women at every level in the organization need to accept. The world is so complex and moving so fast that it is not possible for a few executives "at the top" to make all of the decisions necessary to keep their organizations competitively sharp. Organizations need people at every level with the courage and the skill to step up to leadership opportunities, whether they're formally designated leaders or not.

Leadership—Or Empowerment?

The most successful organizations I know are chock-full of principled, committed people who have been encouraged and prepared to do whatever it takes to help their organizations reach their goals—challenge accepted wisdom, if need be, make independent decisions based on their own assessments, take risks, and continuously be on the alert for those moments when someone needs to step in and keep things moving forward.

Isn't this really just empowerment? I don't think so. To me this is leadership. In fact, it's what any formally designated leader does every day of his or her life. If you allow for issues of scope and scale, it's what every employee in an organization should be able to do. When we call this empowerment, I think we're selling people short. We're saying, in effect, "It's nice to show some initiative. Everybody's overworked these days, and we need people to pitch in and help out. But of course you can't be expected to have the judgment of someone like a supervisor or manager who is in an official position of leadership. So don't go too far. Don't push too hard. Don't care too much."

To Be a Leader

This book is written for those of you who want to make a difference in your organizations regardless of your job title. It will help you understand that:

- Your organization will operate most effectively when its goals are clear, ambitious, and measurable. If they're not, don't sit back and complain. In such circumstances, your greatest leadership opportunity may be to push for clarity.

- Successful leaders tune in to where their organization is going, look around to see what needs to be done to get there, and move quickly to do it. They have a bias for results.

- As a leader, you need a healthy dose of self-confidence. The going will get tough, so you need the inner strength to push ahead.

In other words, this book provides the perspective and the skills people at any level of the organization can use to become more effective leaders. It will help you make a difference.

—Mark H. Willes
Chairman, President, and Chief Executive Officer,
Times Mirror, and
Publisher, *Los Angeles Times*

Because If You Don't, No One Will

BEING A LEADER IN TODAY'S CHANGE-SATURATED ORGANIZATIONS often feels more like picking your way through a torn-up land sprawl full of half-finished construction projects, where freeways end abruptly in midspan, and billboards advertising bright futures compete for your attention with road signs long out of date. As you go along, you see problems that need fixing and people who could possibly use some assistance. You wonder if you should keep moving or if you should stop and help. But then you ask yourself, "If I were to stop, what could I do? What *should* I do?"

This book provides a road map for people who aspire to leadership success in this new world. It describes a breakthrough model of grassroots leadership based on an analysis of hundreds of observed experiences of what people *actually do* when they lead. Made up of specific behaviors that you can learn, this grassroots model applies equally to those in formal management positions and to individual contributors with no positional authority—people who don't really think of themselves as leaders, yet who nevertheless seem to have leadership challenges forced upon them on almost a daily basis. Best observed and most effective in one-on-one and small-group interactions, this kind of leadership is nevertheless not for the faint of heart. It calls for someone with the skills of a salesperson, the credibility of a trusted friend, and occasionally the courage of a freedom fighter.

•   •   •

At 2:30 in the afternoon Tony is facing a challenge he is not sure he is up for.

Tony used to think he was a product development engineer, but now he seems to be "attached" to the Customer Support Center pretty much full-time. He's been there on the phone all day answering customers' questions about one of the sophisticated monitoring systems his company manufactures. It's actually the system he helped design six years ago—the one that got handed off to another manufacturing line last year as part of a big cost-cutting consolidation, where it occupies a low-priority position in the new line's list of products. Not surprisingly, this product now has one of the poorest yield rates of any product in the company. It sometimes seems to Tony that everyone wishes the product would just go away.

Everyone except the customers. At the moment, Tony's on the phone with a salesman who's complaining that he's got six hot orders and can't get Manufacturing to commit to a firm ship date. "Come on, Tony," he wheedles. "Go over there and see if you can't light a fire under somebody."

"Like who? I don't even know half those guys any more."

"But they know you! You're the expert on this product!"

"Look," Tony replies, "as far as they're concerned, all this product has ever done is make them look bad. I've got no time to get in the middle of another fight with them."

"But I got six orders here! You've got to do something!"

"Me!? Why me?"

"Because if you don't," the salesman says, "there's no one who will."

As Tony trudges across the plant to the other line, he is not looking forward to the reception he'll get. He doesn't even know if this is something he should be spending his time on. Maybe he simply feels sorry for the salesman. Maybe he's got too much of himself invested in this product. Maybe the company *is* phasing it out. Tony has asked his boss in Product Development about the possibility but hasn't gotten a straight answer. Besides, Tony now spends so much time in the Support Center he hardly sees his boss any more.

•   •   •

New Opportunities for Leadership

Although the specifics may differ, the dilemma the salesman has dropped in Tony's lap is very much like the leadership challenges faced by all those men and women who are struggling today to make sense out of new ways of working, often in looser corporate configurations that have *un*defined, but not necessarily *re*defined, their jobs. They care about the organization, often very deeply. They've gotten the message about not resisting change, but how do they translate this into action? It's not that they don't see situations where their help seems needed; they see all too many. What they don't see is the support or the authority to intervene. Often, in fact, they run into just the opposite: inertia, covert (and overt) resistance, and messy interpersonal issues, none of which they feel equipped to handle.

The research on which this book is based cuts through this confusion by focusing on the concrete behaviors that were observed to produce leadership. It highlights what leadership actually looks like as it is practiced today, who the real leaders are, and where to concentrate your efforts to be a successful leader yourself. It was written for managers, nonmanagers, team leaders, project managers, and human resource professionals.

Seizing opportunities for grassroots leadership is not a risk-free proposition. Often ambiguous and poorly defined, such opportunities don't come with either a set of instructions from the boss or a promise of absolution if things turn out badly. To be successful, people often have to go outside their departments, as well as their comfort zones. They may need to call policies and procedures into question and force the people higher up in the organization to provide more information, to clarify issues, and to make difficult decisions.

If those opportunities are so challenging, why, then, are people pursuing them? Because they want to make their jobs, and other people's jobs, easier? Feel a strong sense of ownership? Need recognition? Seek advancement? Want to make an impact? Our research indicates it's for all of these reasons, and more. Sometimes, it's out of a heartfelt conviction that it's simply the right thing to do. And sometimes, as for Tony, it's because of a complex interplay of unexamined reasons that the salesman tapped into when he said, "Because if you don't, there's no one who will."

•   •   •

Thinking as he walks along about what he's going to say to the operators, Tony knows that his strongest argument is the continuing customer demand for this product. After all, why is the company in business, if not to provide customers what they want and need? At the same time he realizes that the situation isn't quite so simple. For one thing, "his" product (which is still how he thinks of it) hasn't generated anything like the sales of its three companion monitoring systems, and it probably never will. So maybe moving the product to the new line was not simply to cut costs. Maybe there's a message there. Maybe the salesman's inability to interest anybody in filling his six orders is further handwriting on the wall. On the other hand, the sales force has always maintained that customers prefer to buy all four systems from one vendor, and that if the company discontinued this one system, it would lose sales of the other three. This being the case, as Tony would like to believe, it makes no sense to deep-six his product . . . does it?

Not for the first time Tony considers how much easier his life would be if the company's overall plans and goals were complete and consistent—and cascaded down (as the head of the plant is always saying) to his level. Instead of trying to read the corporate tea leaves, he'd know exactly where he stood, and how he should be spending his time. He remembers a period in the past when his boss could have guided him on these matters, but she's so overloaded these days she doesn't have the time. In fact, Tony has begun to wonder if, even with all the time in the world, she could help him.

In the back of his mind the suspicion is growing that the only way he's going to get answers is to force the issue in some way—although he's not sure how, or with whom. Who knows, this meeting he's about to have could be a step in that direction.

•　　•　　•

What Has Created These Grassroots Leadership Opportunities?

These opportunities have emerged as the result of far-reaching changes taking place in organizations throughout the world.

Increased Competition and More Demanding Customers

Better, faster, cheaper, newer. These are the standards organizations must meet to be competitive today—not just one or two or three of them, but all four. This is a tall order, and in the last decade, organizations have turned themselves inside out trying to reach these goals. Pity the organization that can't figure out how to simultaneously (1) stay ahead of the competition; (2) give its customers not only what they want, but also what they need—plus what they never thought of but will be totally dazzled by once they get it; and oh yes, also (3) make a profit.

A Loosening-Up of the Formal Organizational Structure

It has been clear for several years that the traditional organizational structure—the standard org chart (see Figure 1.1); the top-down chain of command; the well-defined responsibilities for executives, managers, and supervisors—doesn't work very well.

As the competitive need for "better, faster, cheaper, newer" pushed performance to its limits, a discrepancy was revealed between the traditional structure and how work actually gets done. Under such pressure, the traditional structure began to break down (Figure 1.2).

This push probably marked the moment at which your job, whether managerial or not, began to feel out of control. No

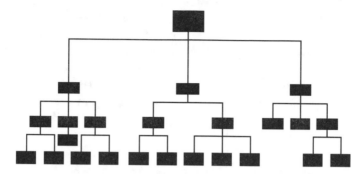

Figure 1.1 The traditional organizational structure.

longer did authority cascade down from the top until it reached you in a compact package of responsibilities that tied neatly into both the level above and the level below yours.

Today, more and more organizations have evolved into structures that resemble a fishnet (see Figure 1.3)—strong, resilient, structured in its way, but flexible enough to drastically change shape depending on the forces applied to it, and the changing goals and directions of the organization.[1]

While you may appreciate the organizational need for such flexibility, if you are in a fishnet organization it is precisely this

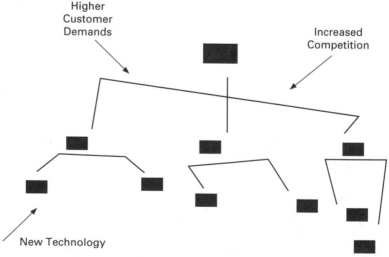

Figure 1.2 The traditional organizational structure under pressure.

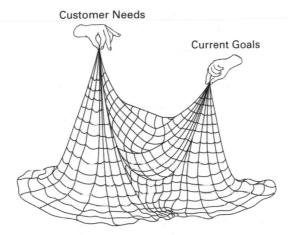

Customer Needs

Current Goals

Figure 1.3 The "fishnet" organization.

flexibility that can drive you crazy. Fishnet organizations still have relationships and hierarchies, but they are temporary, lasting only as long as a task requires them. The structure is constantly being redraped, so to speak, so that exactly the right components can come together to respond to specific and fast-changing business needs. Boundaries between the organization and the rest of the world are deliberately blurred so the organization can get as close as possible to customers, and also enter into outside partnerships and alliances. Although such flexibility may be necessary for business reasons, it can play havoc with your roles and responsibilities, and it offers little guidance about how to structure your contribution to the organization.

Fewer and Busier Managers

Another factor creating new leadership opportunities is the reduction in managerial ranks. Today, there are fewer managers and supervisors than there used to be, and those who are left have been given so many extra responsibilities and people to manage that they can't always carry out their traditional leadership duties. Besides, in today's organizations, there are so many cross-functional teams, so many off-site and outsourced activities, that managers don't have nearly the knowledge of or control over events they once did.

One duty that has fallen victim to this trend is the annual performance evaluation. Never a favorite among managers, in today's cross-functional, long-distance organization this mandated activity can seem truly anachronistic. Take the experience of a research manager, whom we can call Wendy, at a multidivision corporation. One of her direct reports, let's call him Leon, is a research analyst who works in another city. He has spent the last year on a cross-functional team developing standards and software guidelines for certain procedures common to all company divisions. Because Wendy is not involved with this project, she has virtually no direct information about the quality of his work. Yet, the company requires her to conduct an annual evaluation of his performance; Leon, for his part, wants and expects feedback on how he's doing.

In this dilemma lie the seeds of a leadership opportunity for members of Leon's team. Why shouldn't they step in and give him feedback about his performance? In fact, some people would say that feedback about Leon from his peers would probably be more accurate than Wendy's, even if she were managing this project from the office next door to his.

The Predominance of the Knowledge Worker

Information is one of an organization's most valuable assets; knowledge workers are the people who create, analyze, and use it. Knowledge workers are sometimes defined as people who don't make anything tangible. These days, however, even workers on the factory floor often use computers and other information-processing equipment. Knowledge workers today are everywhere—in manufacturing, design, finance, information services, customer service, and technical support. According to the U.S. Bureau of Labor Statistics, between 1986 and 1996 the number of "professional specialty" workers increased by 34 percent, compared with a 19 percent increase in the number of workers in all occupations. Between 1996 and 2006, growth in this category is expected to outstrip total growth in all occupational areas by more than 15 percent.[2]

As a knowledge worker, to some degree you probably share several common characteristics and patterns of work, which have contributed to the creation of new leadership opportunities. Often you work on your own. The work you do and the value you add can be hard to observe, because they involve thought and judgment. You may know more about your work than your manager does. You may feel a stronger allegiance to your academic discipline or field of expertise than to your organization. Finally, although you don't necessarily value management skills or want to move up to a management position, you may become involved in projects and project teams that require you to do management work.

Although knowledge workers tend to be self-managing, at least to the extent that they don't want or need daily supervision, they're not necessarily self-*leading*. They still need the leadership their managers once provided, even if they can't get it from their busy managers any more. They may need coaching to improve their performance. They may need periodic updates to understand how their work fits into changing organizational objectives.

A Growing Focus on Projects and Teams

You've probably noticed a shift in your organization away from managing routine, day-to-day activities toward managing projects. Projects present a raft of leadership challenges: project members from different departments, resources seldom under the direct control of a project manager, and reporting relationships that can create conflicts between project and departmental goals. In addition to project teams, many organizations today have reconfigured departments and work groups into permanent teams, ranging from hierarchical, business-as-usual groups to totally self-managed entities. These new configurations present opportunities for leadership within teams, between teams and the rest of the organization, and between teams and customers and the rest of the outside world.

•   •   •

As Tony drives home that evening after his meeting with the operators on the other line, he realizes that although he still doesn't have answers to any of his big questions, at least a lot of little roadblocks came to light. He wrote them all down. One, the materials aren't being stored properly; no wonder they don't perform up to spec. Two, the line supervisor, who always gets so argumentative about having to change over the line for such a "piddling little run," doesn't really understand the process but has been too embarrassed to admit it. Three, several pallets sat on the receiving dock for two days before anyone noticed them. And so forth. Tony is surprised by the positive reception he got from the operators. Maybe he shouldn't have taken notes. Now they probably think he's going to get things straightened out for them.

•   •   •

What Does Leadership Look Like?

As more employees at every level find themselves, like Tony, almost forced to exercise leadership—the if-you-don't-no-one-will scenario—we at AchieveGlobal have sought to learn more about the skills and behaviors required in such cases, and about current patterns of leadership in general. As a world-wide training and consulting company, we provide training in the skills that help people lead more effectively at *all organizational levels*. We therefore asked, "How do the skills and behaviors required of people like Tony differ from those required of executives, managers, and other nominal leaders? Furthermore, what training will best prepare employees at every level to make the most of these emerging leadership opportunities?"

Before we raised these questions in 1995, most of our leadership research focused on formal leaders at the supervisory, managerial, and executive levels. In the early 1990s, for example, we undertook a study to identify the factors that promoted organizational change. We asked a cross section of executives

in both successful and less successful U.S. and Canadian organizations to describe and rate their own success on 15 dimensions of organizational improvement, including productivity,
cycle time, customer loyalty, profitability, employee retention,
and market share. We compared responses from the successful
with the less successful organizations. What emerged was a
clear picture of what the successful executives did that made
the difference.

We summarized these findings in five key strategies we
called the CLIMB™ model of executive effectiveness, which
became the basis for much of our consulting work with executive teams. The CLIMB model describes the five leadership
strategies that outstanding executives follow to ensure the success of an organizational change initiative:

Create a compelling future.

Let the customer drive the organization.

Involve every mind.

Manage work horizontally.

Build personal credibility.

Then, in 1995, we began the search for skills and behaviors
that might help nonmanagers like Tony meet the less-structured
leadership challenges of today's organization. We launched this
wider search by analyzing over 100 leadership studies and
scores of books on leadership. Our initial findings were, at best,
inconclusive.

- All the studies examined leadership in formal leaders—
  executives and managers—not in technical workers, nonmanagement professionals, project leaders, team leaders,
  and frontline employees. Yet, in today's pared-down organizations, these employees are not only increasing in number, in the absence of traditional managers they are
  precisely the men and women who have leadership virtually foisted on them.

- We found no consensus on what makes a good leader.
  Lists of skills and attributes differed from study to study. It

seemed that every professor, management guru, and strategist had his or her view, and agreement on findings was relatively rare.

- The opinions of survey respondents tended to reflect theories in vogue at the time of a particular study. For example, when Peters and Waterman's best-seller, *In Search of Excellence,* was scoring points in executive boardrooms, over 30 percent of respondents in studies of that period cited "management by walking around" as a desirable leadership behavior. In earlier and later studies, that advice rarely appeared.

- Most studies described leadership in general terms. For instance, although a study might mention integrity as an attribute of effective leaders, researchers rarely explored the day-to-day behaviors or skills that embody or communicate that attribute.

These early efforts helped us see that if we wanted to find a leadership model expressing today's realities, we would have to conduct our own research. We wanted to isolate a set of competencies closely associated with effective leadership, regardless of the level or role of the employee who masters them. To clarify those competencies, we chose the critical-incident methodology, an approach validated in literally thousands of studies since the early 1940s.[3]

Using this methodology, AchieveGlobal researchers asked people at all organizational levels to describe specific recent occurrences of both good and poor leadership that they had observed directly. Incidents could involve managers (supervisors, middle management, and executives) or nonmanagers (e.g., technical workers, nonmanagement professionals, project leaders, team leaders, and frontline employees).

What We Asked

Think of a time within the past month when a person in your organization showed good (or poor) leadership. What did that person do that showed good (or poor) leadership? What was the result of this behavior? What was the person's position in your organization?

We simply asked our respondents to recall an incident and describe what happened as clearly as possible. Later, we sorted the incidents into categories based on the central behavior, purpose, or result described in each incident.

Our study engaged the full organizational hierarchy, from corporate executive officers (CEOs) and government executives to frontline employees in over 450 organizations (randomly chosen from growth sectors like manufacturing, high-tech, service, government, and education) in all major regions of the United States and Canada. Organizations ranged in size from fewer than 250 employees to over 10,000. The study produced 1,871 critical incidents—verbal snapshots, as it were—of what individuals in a range of roles and industries regarded as examples of leadership, or its absence. Researchers then analyzed the incidents for commonalities, sorted them into 120 larger *categories of behavior,* and combined closely related categories into 17 *leadership competencies.* Figure 1.4 illustrates that process.

A New Grassroots Model of Leadership

We believe that the leadership competencies we identified add up to a new *grassroots model of leadership,* derived from and appropriate to a range of roles at all organizational levels. The critical-incident approach allows us to define leadership based on the day-to-day actions of individuals, as described by other individuals, at every level of the organization. In that respect, this model differs from leadership models resting solely on the experiences and opinions of designated leaders, or on what

CRITICAL INCIDENTS	CATEGORIES OF BEHAVIOR	COMPETENCY
"Convinced management to present reorganization in the company newsletter."	Makes strategic databases available to all workers	
"Set up department meeting to discuss impending reorganization."	Keeps people informed of significant internal events	Shares information
"Set up filing system."		

Figure 1.4 Example: from critical incidents to competency.

experts say leaders should do. We call it a *grassroots* model of leadership because it's rooted in behaviors that can be performed by anyone regardless of position.

The following 17 competencies in the model add up to what leadership looks like:

1. Create and describe a vision.
2. Manage changes required to realize a vision.
3. Respond to identified customer needs.
4. Support individual effort.
5. Support team effort.
6. Share information.
7. Make decisions that solve problems.
8. Manage cross-functional processes.
9. Display technical skills.
10. Manage projects.
11. Manage time and resources.
12. Take initiative beyond job requirements.
13. Take responsibility for your own actions and the actions of your group.
14. Handle emotions in yourself and others.
15. Display professional ethics.
16. Show compassion.
17. Make credible presentations.

These competencies define leadership as behaviors—not as traits such as tenacity, for example, or integrity, which are often held to be key characteristics of effective leaders. The distinction between a behavior and a trait is important to anyone who wants to become a better leader. It's possible through study and practice to learn specific behaviors, like "share information," but acquiring a trait like "openness," for example, or "honesty" is a far more daunting task. We have found that the best way to acquire a trait is to learn the behaviors that express it. For this reason, the grassroots model is not only more reality-based than more theoretical constructs, it's also more learnable.

The Leader in Each of Us

Still, our research prompted a key question: Do we need a new summary model of leadership for nonmanagement staff, or will the CLIMB model serve to guide this group as well as executives? To answer that question, we enlisted both Achieve-Global and outside researchers to review the critical incidents and the competencies through the lens of the CLIMB strategies. With strong agreement among independent researchers, we were able to associate each of the incidents and competencies with one of the five CLIMB strategies as follows:

CLIMB STRATEGIES	COMPETENCIES
Create a compelling future.	Create and describe a vision.
	Manage changes required to realize a vision.
Let the customer drive the organization.	Respond to identified customer needs.
Involve every mind.	Support individual effort.
	Support team effort.
	Share information.
	Make decisions that solve problems.
Manage work horizontally.	Manage cross-functional processes.
	Display technical skills.
	Manage projects.
	Manage time and resources.
Build personal credibility.	Take initiative beyond job requirements.
	Take responsibility for your own actions and the actions of your group.
	Handle emotions in yourself and others.
	Display professional ethics.
	Show compassion.
	Make credible presentations.

Because the critical incidents describe people at every level, the CLIMB model defines leadership not just for executives, but for *every* employee. Using CLIMB, it's possible to evaluate leadership using the very same criteria for the executive as for the frontline worker. More important, it's possible to improve leadership at all levels by training people in the competencies summarized in CLIMB.

In other words, there is a leader in each of us—if we master and apply the CLIMB strategies—whether we're president, sales manager, technician, or staff support person.

Other Key Findings

In addition to identifying the competencies of leadership, the critical-incident study produced the following key findings—some new, and some important affirmations of earlier thinking.

Organizations today cannot survive if leadership is limited to the CEOs, executives, and managers.   Life moves too quickly, and top management is too removed from the action. As the incidents demonstrated, leadership opportunities can arise at any moment:

- On a busy loading dock when a foreman switches carriers because he reads of an impending strike

- During a heated team meeting when one of the members takes it upon him- or herself to mediate the dispute

- When a harried administrative assistant volunteers to pull in extra people to get a proposal out on time

People define leaders by what they do—or don't do—in "small" moments.   Respondents in the study talked about people who took a moment to coach, to bolster confidence, to resolve a dispute, or to go after a resource. This is in marked contrast to the commonly held belief that leaders define themselves through heroic, high-profile actions.

The instant that people experience you as a leader, they start keeping score.   It's not clear why, but the study found that if you step up to a leadership challenge, people will judge you as a leader not only in that situation, but from that point on. Their criteria: how well you perform the 17 competencies.

For people to see you as a leader, you need the complete set of leadership skills.   Just as strength in one or two academic subjects does not make a good student, in the eyes of the respondents strength in a few leadership competencies does not make a good leader.

How the Book Is Organized

Each of the five main chapters of the book focuses on one of the five CLIMB strategies and covers:

1. Why it's important
2. Symptoms to watch for in your work group or organization that indicate the strategy is being badly executed or underexecuted
3. What you can do to carry it out successfully
4. Examples of how leaders at all organizational levels have applied it
5. Reference to specific tools and techniques to help you perform this strategy (see Tools: Grassroots Leadership Step by Step and the appendices)

The appendices also contain additional background on the AchieveGlobal research supporting this book, and in addition you'll find a bibliography of pertinent books and articles.

•   •   •

The clock next to the bed says 2:00 A.M. Tony turns over and tries to go back to sleep, but his mind refuses to slow down. Forget about it, he tells himself. There's no way you can take those operators under your wing, absolutely no way. Five minutes later he gives up on sleeping and pads downstairs to see what's in the refrigerator. With considerable misgivings, he realizes he's in too far to back out now. Nobody cares as much as he does. It's not fair, he thinks. If work keeps you from sleeping, at least it ought to be your own work.

•   •   •

Grassroots Leadership Step by Step

Look Inside: How Good a Leader Are You? In the tools section on pages 129–132, you will find a leadership profile based on the five CLIMB strategies. Completing this self-evaluation will give you an idea of how you rate your own performance as a leader according to the criteria that the critical-incident study showed others will use to judge you.

From breakthrough research, AchieveGlobal has developed a new model of leadership that applies equally to managers and nonmanagers. The model emerges from, and is geared to, changes that have swept across organizations in the last decade: a loosening of structure, fewer and busier managers, more knowledge workers, and a growing focus on projects and teams. What makes it a grassroots model is the fact that it's based on a collection of hundreds of actual incidents—verbal snapshots—in which people at all organizational levels demonstrated behavior that was described by direct observers as leadership. From this research emerged a series of 17 leadership competencies—specific behaviors that anyone can learn to become a more effective leader at any level of the organization. Furthermore, these were found to correlate closely with AchieveGlobal's five CLIMB strategies for executive effectiveness.

2

Create a Compelling Future

The competencies that support this strategy are "Create and describe a vision," and "Manage changes required to realize a vision." Only 7% of all the critical incidents fall into this strategy. This finding contrasts sharply with other leadership research in which vision is mentioned more frequently.

THIS IS THE DIMENSION OF LEADERSHIP THAT PEOPLE MOST OFTEN cite as "what leaders do." Although for many people "creating a compelling future" evokes images of high-powered executives sitting around conference tables devising strategies and hammering out vision statements, this is not the picture that emerged from our research. The leadership behaviors that made enough of an impression for people to remember and describe to our researchers were more interpersonal. They included: "clearly articulates goals or plans," "becomes personally involved," "plans for the change," "invites participation by others in shaping the vision," "actively supports the change," "shares information and doesn't leave others in the dark," "takes time to see where specific individuals fit in," and "helps people see the importance of the goal."

Each of these incidents represents a small moment, in most cases involving only a few people. Nevertheless, each moment was pivotal, in that during this brief time some desired future state either moved a step or two closer to reality or was side-tracked. Those who wonder why it's so difficult for their organizations to carry out a new strategy or move in a different direction might start by taking a look at these incidents. Moreover, many of the behaviors that made a difference, either positively or negatively, did not require substantial resources or high-level authority. In other words, they were—or could have been—performed by individual contributors.

Why didn't the more strategic, cerebral leadership activities show up in the critical incidents? It's not because people think they are unimportant; a more likely reason is that they are simply not so frequently or easily observed as these more personal interactions. The lesson for top leadership may be that, if they expect their organization's vision for the future to take hold, they need to get out of their offices, make more of an effort to personalize their vision, and encourage others to do the same.

A big part of creating a compelling future is translating high-level vision statements into concepts and images that resonate with the people you're talking to. The most effective leaders do not necessarily try to take the magic out of these statements, or focus only on explaining what they really mean. These leaders know that compelling futures are not created from facts alone; they must incorporate words and images that resonate with people's dreams and hopes as well.

With a future that they find compelling—a word the dictionary defines as "drivingly forceful"—people will overlook problems and press on through frustration and confusion that would otherwise defeat them. According to our research, people who see a future for themselves will forgive almost anything; without a future, they will forgive almost nothing. Forgiveness is never more needed than during a change initiative or organizational regrouping, when chaos reigns and everyone is stretched to the breaking point. At times like these, a manager may not always be available to rally the troops. There's no reason, however, that an individual contributor can't step up to the challenge. That's what happened in a United Kingdom plant that was launching a process improvement initiative. One member of a product development team had been on an earlier team that had worked hard to establish consistency in the development process. She took it upon herself to sell the benefits of consistency to her new team, with the result that other team members bought into the idea, the process went more smoothly, and the need for management involvement was reduced.

For today's questioning and skeptical knowledge workers, the need for a future they can believe in is especially critical. Without a vision that makes sense to them, these independent men and women will essentially go their own way, sometimes to the detriment of the organization, and the leader is left running just to catch up. "There are times when I feel like a shepherd," said Anthony O'Dowd, vice president of international product development for COREL Corporation Ltd. in Ireland, "and not a very good one at that. I manage to get three sheep in the pen, but as soon as I go off to get the others the first three escape."

Before you can create a compelling future for other people, you may first have to resolve your own confusion and uncertainty, and come up with a future you can feel good about. Sometimes, you may have to force the issue. A field service engineer, caught between requests for help from customers and a seemingly uninterested management, arranged for a conference call among himself, his boss, and his most vociferous customer. "He broke the logjam," wrote a fellow engineer. "The manager saw the problem, and the decisions that had to be made."

When the Future Does Not Seem Compelling— Or Even Clear

A certain amount of complaining about top management is a normal part of organizational life, but if you hear—or think to yourself—comments like the following too often, the mood in your organization or work group may have slipped from harmless bellyaching to paralyzing skepticism:

- "I'm not against change per se, but this makes no sense at all!"
- "An all-day meeting to plan for the next quarter? If we don't get this done right now, there won't *be* a next quarter."
- "Why bother?"
- "Just tell me what to do, and I'll do it."
- "Sometimes I think I ought to look for a job with a company that knows where it's going."

If no one steps in to stop this slide, your organization will eventually stall out on its efforts to change and grow. In people terms, the result is more than lack of motivation. It's the anxiety that comes from doubting or not knowing the direction you're taking ("People are unhappy; There is high turnover;" "It sets things up for failure;" and "Momentum is lost.").

The critical incidents in this chapter illuminate the impact of both the negative and positive behaviors. By observing where the successful leaders concentrate their efforts, we have distilled a series of best practices—the key areas successful grassroots leaders concentrate on to create a compelling future.

A Word on the Critical Incidents

All the critical incidents in this book, taken from the AchieveGlobal study, are examples of specific leadership behaviors, good and not-so-good, observed *by* employees *of* other employees at all levels of their organizations. Think of them as a series of candid, verbal snapshots taken when their subjects were caught in the act of being themselves. Because they're unposed, so to speak, these snapshots tell us which behaviors people actually think of as leadership behavior (versus what they might have read or been told) and how they judge these behaviors. The critical incidents are augmented with examples taken from subsequent interviews by the authors of men and women in the United States, Canada, Australia, Ireland, and Great Britain who confront leadership issues in their own work.

In these pages we will be highlighting the patterns that emerge from these snapshots in the hopes of shortening the learning curve of all those readers who are interested in knowing how to become effective grassroots leaders.

How Grassroots Leaders Create a Compelling Future

Our study indicates there are four key areas in which successful grassroots leaders concentrate their efforts—best practices, so to speak, which both managers and nonmanagers follow to create a compelling future.

1. They help others personalize a future for themselves.
2. They navigate through emotional ups and downs.
3. They're not afraid of midcourse adjustments.
4. They find a way to maintain a sense of optimism.

The image of a person who is most successful at this strategy might be that of a highly skilled and ethical salesperson, someone who is deeply convinced of the benefits of what he or she is selling, and is able to evoke these benefits in a way that other people can internalize as their own.

Grassroots Leaders Help Others Personalize a Future for Themselves

When all is said and done, what people want is to know how a corporate vision or future direction will affect their lives. They want to know what's in it for them, of course, but they also want to know how their own lives will be different, what sacrifices they must make, and what the eventual payoff may be. They need the chance to look at this vision from all angles, to poke and prod a little, and to hold it against them to see how it fits. It's difficult to see how such needs could be met at arm's length—by means of a corporate video, for example, or an official vision statement. Behind the negative critical incidents about absent leaders and managers who spent too much time off by themselves were pleas for more of this kind of hands-on involvement. "Our day-to-day work gets done," said one member of a management team, "but there is no sense that we are working for the same goals. Roles are not clear in the department; there is a factionalism and an overall confusion about what is expected. The leader shuts himself off from some of his managers who could really help him organize his thoughts about the future. There is no teamwork in our department. We are set up for failure."

The power of personal involvement emerges in a critical incident from a financial services institution, in which a leader participated with other employees in the process of writing a vision statement. Said the respondent, "Our senior VP brought together a cross section of his organization, managers through nonexempt staff, to write a vision statement for the organization. He participated as an equal with everyone on the staff. The participation of each person was full and complete. Consequently, people felt listened to. They sensed that regardless of rank, they were able to contribute their ideas and experience. The result was complete ownership as they made themselves 'vision ambassadors' for the new statement."

If you can get people to think of themselves as vision ambassadors for a future you've created, you've really done your job.

Paint a Picture, Put Others in It—And Then Give Them the Paint Brush

In one of the most powerful critical incidents, someone described a successful leader as "painting a picture of his vision so clearly that I could see myself in it." Another person wrote, "Our vice president made me believe [our vision] couldn't happen without me." In yet another example, an employee confided, "We were able to see just exactly where we fit in."

Successful leaders realize that for a compelling future to take hold, it must become everyone's future, not just theirs. As a grassroots leader, your job is not to keep the vision pure, but to encourage others to internalize it as their own. If you have a need to create a future based only on your own ideas, chances are slim that others will find your future as drivingly forceful as they would if you'd helped them make it theirs as well as yours.

Giving others a chance to paint themselves into the picture of the future can take time. If there's an urgent need to move ahead quickly—and sometimes there is—it's tempting to skip over this part of the strategy. Balancing the need for involvement with the need for fast results is a tough judgment call, and it's possible to err on either side. Perhaps the most useful advice is simply to be aware of the hidden costs of meeting a deadline under pressure. These were apparent in the following incident involving the blending of two e-mail systems into one, following a corporate merger. "How the transition would be made, and when, was decided solely by management," an employee from Information Services wrote. "They just said, 'We want it done by June 15th.' People in MIS were never asked what the best solution would be for our two companies. We were never told why they wanted to have everybody on one system so quickly. We were simply told, 'This is it. We can't move the date back.' "

Predictably, the push for a speedy implementation produced substantial delays, along with some hard feelings. "Honestly, I wanted to quit for a period of time because nobody would tell us anything," she continued. "I fought it at first and didn't get anywhere, so then I said, 'If you can't fight the enemy, join them, and be part of the enemy,' which I have. But I've got a cold now. It's probably from not sleeping all week."

Another way to start painting a new picture of the future is to get people thinking about what's wrong with the old one. This was the approach taken by an operator on a manufacturing team in the United Kingdom, which was charged with reducing cycle time. "He looked at all the items we had on the shop floor and started asking people questions about them," the respondent said. " 'Where did they come from? How long had they been there?' He caused other people to get interested in how it ought to be. Of course, that led to all sorts of things happening."

Avoid the "Leaderly" Trap

There seems to be something about "the vision thing" that can trigger "leaderly," father-knows-best behavior in people who otherwise work collaboratively. This may be what happened to a manager who pounced on a newly issued corporate vision statement and ran with it. Possibly eager to get some recognition for himself and his team, he asked the people in his department to come up with radical new ideas over the weekend that could save the company money. The following Monday he held a follow-up meeting, during which he talked about his own ideas and never got around to asking his subordinates about theirs. He may have simply wanted to show that he was on top of things, but he completely demotivated his group, and would probably be surprised at how negatively the group members judged his behavior. Said one, "It's clear that the manager wants all the control and that our ideas aren't valued. Afterwards, one person who had spent a lot of time on the weekend coming up with suggestions was incensed about having wasted all those hours generating ideas she couldn't present. I'd be surprised if anybody in the department cares any more about saving money or responding to any other corporate issue."

Overcommunicate

Employees at all levels need plenty of time to internalize the impact of corporate change on what they do. You can't assume that presenting the vision once, either in a written communication, videotaped speech, or at a meeting, means that people will get it. That's like saying that one strong press of the gas pedal is all it takes to get you to your destination. After you give your car enough gas to overcome initial inertia, you must still keep your foot on the accelerator to maintain your speed. You've got to keep pushing—and recommunicating. The point at which you're driving yourself crazy is probably the point at which people will *start* to hear what you're saying. It might help to keep in mind that when you present a change initiative or new strategy, you may have been working with it for some time. Don't forget how long it might have taken you to accept the concepts you now want others to take in.

Often, the real impact of a major change sinks in slowly; you have to be prepared to revisit issues you thought you'd laid to rest. This happened to an in-house designer (let's call her Lois) who was given the assignment of creating a new corporate look for all of her company's publications. "The vision was to come up with a new page layout design for new products," she said in an interview, "but we soon realized we had a much larger opportunity in front of us—namely, to establish a new company-wide standard that would affect other areas of business, such as customization and translations."

Lois involved the appropriate people from across the company. Although everyone liked the idea at first, she says, as the project has progressed people have begun to realize just exactly how much this new vision will affect their operations, and what they may have to give up as a result. When they reach this point their enthusiasm almost evaporates. "Getting them to maintain their commitment and participation isn't easy," she said. "I periodically have to sell them again, and at those times, it feels like I'm starting from scratch.

"This is taking a lot longer than I thought it would. It's all about getting people enthusiastic and getting them to stay for the whole ride. It's a constant sell. But there are benefits to all this individual hand-holding. It's allowed me to build stronger personal bridges with many people. They're starting to feel they have an actionable part in what's going on, and that they'll be an integral part of those decisions."

Seize the Moment

Some of the most effective communication these days takes place not in formal meetings but in quick, unplanned casual encounters: on the elevator, in the parking lot, outside someone's office. These brief moments should be put to good use; they may be the only moments available. Here's how a department head at an insurance company made creative use of an informal gathering. "He just dropped in while a group of us were sitting around talking sales strategy, and helped us relate the new corporate mission to the issues at hand. He listened and showed interest in our ideas and concerns, and asked for and invited questions which left us feeling impressed, inspired, and valued. Hearing what we had to say reminded him how easy it is for a manager to get out of touch. He consequently invited all employees to memo him whenever they had important issues that needed to be aired."

In another critical incident the head of a department had held a big meeting to discuss a change. Unfortunately, she was on the road most of the time and hard to reach for one-on-one or group follow-up discussions, so to make herself as available as possible she circulated a memo to her staff, which said, "You can call me on voice mail, on e-mail or by phone. And if you want to dialogue as a group, I've scheduled two slots during the week when I'll be available for conference calls."

Deal Directly with the Downside

Major upheavals like downsizing and mergers don't always bring good news. Still, the positive incidents in our study indicate that people find the facts less immobilizing than the fears engendered by fact-free speculation. Leaders may dread being the bearers of bad tidings, but if they're straightforward, and make themselves available to answer questions, people can handle the news. Furthermore, they will respect the leaders for putting themselves on the line. One department was rife with rumors about layoffs and the introduction of new technology nobody knew anything about. The leader explained the competitive pressures that had necessitated drastic action. As the respondent said, "He painted a vision for all to understand, and made an honest appeal for all to open up their minds to new processes, new technology. . . . People walked away understanding the direction that has to be taken in our competitive environment."

In other cases, managers get ambitious performance goals dumped on them, and simply turn around and dump them on others. Preestablished goals are a fact of life, and people need to discuss and understand them even if they have no input in them. Leaders who duck a full discussion for fear they'll appear powerless ("I don't agree either, but what can I do?"), or because they don't want to deal with complaints and bad feelings might want to keep the following incident in mind, which occurred during a critical transitional period. The director of a business unit failed to communicate openly with his team. "The goals the director presented to our team were unusually daunting," one team member said, "but he never bothered to articulate their importance or create an opportunity for us to discuss them. So we never understood what they really meant. There was no opportunity to raise questions, clarify issues, and test our understanding of the changes that were taking place. Consequently, there was a lot of grumbling and discontent. Considering people's lack of understanding, there's not a snowball's chance in hell that we'll meet these goals."

Grassroots Leaders Navigate through Emotional Ups and Downs

One way to know if your message about a compelling future is getting through to people is to tune in to the emotional component in their reactions. Any significant change in our lives is likely to trigger responses that are not completely rational or adult. It's a little like when we were children and creaked open a door into a darkened room. Until the light flicked on, we were likely to project all kinds of terrible things lurking in the dark. Change can feel a little like that. A familiar structure has been dismantled, but nobody is yet sure what the new order is all about. That's when people are at their most vulnerable. Imagine, for example, how you would feel if you were any of the following people:

- A sales rep whose salary will now be based not on his performance, but on how well his whole region performs and the ability of the group to cross-sell a new line of products.

- A financial analyst who must now work with data from additional departments who use different software.

- A member of a department who will move from individual cubicles to a single common office as part of an initiative to establish work teams.

- The director of product engineering in a company that has set itself the goal of becoming less product- and more market-driven.

At times like these, people demonstrate leadership by being patient, and by understanding that these situations may activate irrational fears and concerns, some of which may need to be aired. In the following incident, the respondent's gratitude for his understanding leader comes through loud and clear: "Our administrator took all the time we needed to explain why restructuring was inevitable. He described his vision for the organization and asked us to help in refining it. He answered all our questions. We now have a clearer understanding of our mission and are able to see where we fit in it. We also understand where and why we have to change. He evoked an atmosphere in which people felt free to ask the questions that really mattered to them. As a result, panic was avoided."

Keep Your Cool

During periods of change clear thinking is often in short supply. Little problems seem like big problems. Frustrated employees grouse about management and wonder why, if the new vision is so great, they can't even get their e-mail to work. Emotions are raw; people can flare up, sink into resentment, lapse into rebellion, boil over in frustration, and, as a last resort, give up and look for employment elsewhere.

Anthony O'Dowd described what happened when he let emotions get the better of him during a company restructuring. What set him off was the decision to move one of the teams reporting to him to another town. "I fought tooth and nail to keep that team in Dublin," he said. "I felt I was correct, and I was passionate about it, but still I lost the fight. Only later, when I heard that people were calling me an empire-builder, did I realize I had let my emotions get the better of me. When people think you're an empire-builder they're saying you don't have good business judgment. As a manager you need to learn to be pragmatic, or at least to seem pragmatic."

Leverage the Ways People Respond to Change

By means of reassurance, patience, and a constant stream of information, leaders can minimize these upheavals. However, to maintain their sanity and everyone else's, leaders need to be prepared for the various predictable ways people react to change, and to know how to make the most of these reactions.

There are four classic responses to change. Some people seem to have an affinity for a particular response, although over a period of time it's not uncommon to move from one response to another. If you're trying to get a change initiative off the ground, you may have little patience for these responses, but in fact they can be useful. (You may also recognize yourself in some of them.)

> **The victim mode.**　Victims wear invisible T-shirts that say, "Why do these things always happen to me?" People who adopt this mode tend to see the change focused exclusively on themselves and feel totally overwhelmed by it. The anger and depression they show often mask more profound feelings of fear and helplessness. Victims often isolate themselves and fail to ask for help.

> **The critic mode.**　Poll a critic, and he or she will say, "This will never work." Although critics appear more rational than victims, they too may harbor unspoken concerns and fears. Critics handle these feelings by focusing on what's wrong. They are constantly on the lookout for any evidence that proves their point; they don't pay much attention to outcomes that are even potentially positive.

> **The bystander mode.**　Bystanders adopt the strategy of passive resistance to change. Reluctant to get involved, they wait for others to make decisions and take the lead. Bystanders watch the game from the sidelines. If they carried signs, these would read, "We're just looking, thanks."

Although these three modes may reflect certain ingrained internal patterns, they can also be appropriate and useful responses to external realities.

- Major change initiatives aren't always made with employees' individual needs in mind. In such cases, the "good soldiers" in the group can benefit from someone in the victim mode who is willing to complain.

- Few change initiatives are perfectly conceived or executed. If your company hasn't done adequate planning, for example, it may benefit from someone—perhaps yourself—moving into the critic mode to raise a red flag and insist on getting better information before moving forward.

- When making a change, there are often strong pressures to act without thinking. Someone in the bystander mode can help create time for people to reflect on what they're doing.

The navigator mode.   This is the most effective mode for someone leading a change. As a navigator, you're certainly not a mindless change advocate, but you do feel confident enough not to be threatened by a disruption of the status quo. You're clear about and comfortable with your own feelings about the change, both positive and negative. You focus on the facts: why the change is needed, the benefits it can produce, and the likely trade-offs involved. You seek out opportunities for improvement and ways to help minimize the negative reactions of others. If you wore a button, it would say, "We can make this work."

Through patience and a willingness to provide reassurance and information, navigators can help victims, bystanders, and critics move on to the navigator mode. In one critical incident, the marketing staff of a manufacturing division benefited from having a leader who operated from the navigator mode during a division reorganization. "During this time, she continued to develop staff and the group, formed task forces, involved everyone, heard out everybody's concerns, and didn't just go off on her own," wrote a member of the group. "This reorganization could have triggered a lot of problems, but instead, she used the reorganization to make everybody grow."

Grassroots Leaders Aren't Afraid of Midcourse Adjustments

It's funny about a compelling future: once other people buy in, they may get their own ideas about how best to carry it out, and these ideas might just be different from yours. If you're in a formal leadership position, you should consider these ideas a sign of your success at creating a future that others care enough about to suggest improvements in. If you're an individual contributor who sees a better way to make something happen, speak up. This is your chance to exercise some grassroots leadership.

Act on Your Convictions

It can be an energizing experience. A product developer from corporate headquarters was launching a new product to regional sales forces throughout the country. At every meeting people had complaints they wanted her to take back to headquarters. They told her they couldn't get anyone there to pay any attention; maybe they'd pay attention to her. "After I finished laughing at that," she said, "I told them if they thought some procedure wasn't working, they should just fix it. If they sit around waiting for permission, nothing will happen. The ones who decided to act got this look in their eyes, like 'OK, it's time for action.' I could feel the energy."

Stay Open to Other Possibilities

If, as a manager, you end up on the receiving end of a challenge to a procedure or directive, you can do yourself a lot of good by keeping an open attitude. Maybe your initial plan needs to be revised; most do. Maybe the approach was wrong. Maybe *you* were wrong, and there is another, better way to do it. Although many people, especially executives and managers, assume that to appear strong and worth following they must have all the answers, our research shows that when people are willing to admit mistakes, learn from them, and move on, they are seen by others as both more credible and more "followable."

Of course, organizations can't succeed by adopting an anything-goes philosophy. The key to being open to other possibilities is always to maintain a laser-beam focus on the desired outcome you want to achieve. "If someone's got a better idea than mine for getting the results, fine," said an executive from the aviation industry. "Results are what I'm interested in. Besides, there are so many measuring sticks people use to judge you, I can guarantee you'll always be wrong according to at least one of them."

Yet, in the real world there are mistakes—and then there are *mistakes.* "It's OK to make mistakes, but you've got to keep them small," this executive said. "The way you do that is to be known as the kind of person who can be talked into another way of doing things. Then people will come to you and you can make the necessary adjustments along the way. If people are afraid of you—or if you are too rigid to accept feedback—and you crash and burn, you'll burn alone. Then you'll get *all* the blame."

Sometimes it takes a particularly dedicated and persistent individual contributor to force the issue with management. In one critical incident, for example, the managers of an insurance company had made an underwriting decision that the field staff knew would not be well received by customers. Nevertheless, most of the staff sat on their hands, because they didn't think the managers would change their minds—except for one person, a marketing sales rep. She took it upon herself to educate the managers as to why their decision was not in the best interests of the customers. Her colleagues were sure she'd made a career-damaging move, but management admitted its mistake, rescinded its decision, and earned the respect of the staff. The message the managers' behavior communicated to the staff was, "We can admit and learn from our mistakes. You, on the other hand, must be willing to take the risk of speaking up."

Grassroots Leaders Find a Way to Maintain a Sense of Optimism

Most of the critical incidents for this strategy focus on tough situations in which the obstacles were considerable, and the chance of eventual success was by no means guaranteed. Yet the leaders in the positive incidents still seem to maintain an optimistic outlook that carries them forward, and that eventually has a positive impact on the people they work with.

Lois, for example, has become very much aware of the challenges involved in getting people to agree on a new corporate look for all publications, but she still believes the benefits will be worth the effort. "I knew there would be some resistance, but I had no idea how much and the magnitude of emotion," she said. "Still, I have to believe that even though there'll be pain and frustration at the beginning, in the long run it'll be easier for everyone . . . and that it will benefit the company, both in the time and cost of producing products."

Balance Pain with Gain

Like Lois, leaders maintain their optimism by constantly balancing present pain against future gain. At the outset of the project, Lois saw the advantages to be gained from a single corporate look, and so far the problems, although greater than she expected, don't outweigh the benefits. On the other hand, if you don't have a clear sense of your organization's vision for the future, you may need to get some more data before you can create a compelling future about which you can be honestly optimistic. In these cases, it sometimes makes sense to focus on a more limited world where you do feel some control. "We may not know exactly what's going on in the rest of the organization," you may say in effect, "but if we follow this path we'll feel good about what we're doing, and the chances are good that it'll be good for the company."

Behave Optimistically

Should you fake optimism you don't feel? Probably not. Over time, most people will see through your act and feel manipulated by it. Worse, they might come to doubt your sincerity in other areas as well. One response is to say nothing. "I have bad days when none of this makes sense," said one project leader. "On those days I try to find private work to do, or I just keep my mouth shut. My attitude usually improves in a day or two. If I stay down, I know I have some rethinking to do."

When a regional vice president of sales for a publishing organization feels self-doubt taking over, she stops and does a quick self-assessment. "Do I have the skills I need?" she asks. "The support? Or am I simply exhausted? I may talk the situation over with a mentor or a friend. If the problem is none of the above, and I still feel down, then all I can do is try to behave in an optimistic way. I'm a firm believer that if you change your behavior, you can change the way you think and feel. *Acting* optimistic can jump-start your mind into *feeling* optimistic. For example, I used to hate the thought of exercise. So I just forced myself to start exercising, and now I love it."

Grassroots Leadership Step by Step

The following leadership tools can help you master some of the more difficult aspects of creating a compelling future. Each of these tools has been thoroughly tested, and has proved its worth in real-life leadership situations. You'll find these in the section called "Tools: Grassroots Leadership Step by Step" (pages 133–143).

Navigating Change (Tool 2).   This tool helps you assess the impact of a change on yourself and others, maximize your ability to adapt successfully, and develop a plan for working most effectively with others (pages 133–135).

The Big Picture (Tool 3).   This tool helps you develop a brief statement-as-sound-bite that succinctly encapsulates your organization's vision or purpose, and how your department or team fits into this larger picture. Once you have prepared this statement, you'll be surprised at how many times you'll use it: when making formal presentations, giving progress reports, answering questions, and in casual conversations with others inside or outside your group or organization. You may also be surprised at how articulate you'll sound on a topic that can be difficult to communicate clearly and memorably (pages 136–138).

How's It Going—Really? (Tool 4).   This tool helps you take advantage of brief moments—in the hall, on an elevator—to find out how someone is coping with a change.

Chances are the information you'll get will be more reliable and also more timely than you would get from a formal meeting. No one has time for lengthy meetings any more. Besides, people are often reluctant to reveal too much in a public setting. What's more, because this tool is so brief, you're likely to use it more often (pages 139–141).

Reframe It! (Tool 5). This tool provides a step-by-step process to help someone who is frustrated with a change look at that event or problem in a different, more positive way. Without telling someone what to do or think, you suggest a point of view that helps the other person make choices to support the goal or strategy in question (pages 142–143).

Unlike popular conceptions of "the vision thing" and the leader as a lonely visionary, the critical incidents cumulatively define this strategy in terms of personal interactions, small moments that nevertheless make the difference between organizational commitment and focus on the one hand, and lack of direction, wasted effort, and self-doubt on the other. Grassroots leaders are seen as people who can create a compelling future for others partly because they aren't afraid of hands-on involvement and frequent communication, even when they don't have all the answers. The specific best practices they follow are:

1. They help others personalize a future for themselves.

2. They navigate through emotional ups and downs.

3. They're not afraid of midcourse adjustments.

4. They find a way to maintain a sense of optimism.

CHAPTER

Let the Customer Drive the Organization

Less than 4% of all the incidents reported in our study make up the single competency ("Act on behalf of the customer"), which supports this strategy. This is the lowest proportion of incidents associated with any of the five strategies.

THIS IS THE CLIMB STRATEGY MOST IN NEED OF AMPLIFICATION. IF WE are to believe the critical incidents, leaders aren't performing the kind of behavior that directly or indirectly puts customers in the driver's seat. As a result, the need to "let the customer drive the organization" may remain for many organizations a worthy, but largely abstract, leadership concept, and therefore less likely to capture mind-share in the way the other, more visible components of leadership do.

What the low number of critical incidents for this strategy tells us is that when people are asked to think of leadership, they don't often think of "acting on behalf of the customer," let alone the higher-level strategy of "letting the customer drive the organization." This is not to say they don't witness incidents every day in which both nonmanagers and managers act with the customer in mind. However, few people within these organizations seem to associate the behaviors required to support a customer orientation with leadership work.

Because we know that what makes leadership real for people is behavior, not concepts, what we can say is that people aren't being exposed to much in the way of memorable, emotionally engaging leadership directed at "letting the customer drive the organization."

The message implied in all this for grassroots leaders is, DO MORE. Despite everything organizations have done in recent years to streamline their operations and get closer to their customers, few seem to have effectively embraced "let the customer drive the organization" as a guiding strategy. We suspect that for employees without direct customer contact, customers remain somewhat vague and shadowy entities, known mostly through out-of-date sales figures and occasional survey data. Corporate slogans to the contrary notwithstanding, too many people still think of serving the customer as something that harassed and heroic frontline employees do, saving everyone else in the organization from having to perform such difficult and exhausting work. In fact, we think that if they were being completely honest, many, if not most, employees would admit that they are far more distracted by and drawn to the internal dynamics of their own departments or work groups than they are to the needs and concerns of their organizations' customers. (To test this claim, it might be interesting to walk around your organization for an hour or so, log the topics of all the conversations you hear, and see how many of them are about customers.)

In saying this, we are only too aware of the other competing claims on people's time and energy—to keep costs down, turn out work more quickly, and so forth. Nor do we mean to shortchange the tremendous improvements organizations have made in customer service in recent years. As a result of their progress, in fact, we as consumers have been conditioned to expect more,

and when we don't get what we expect, we demand it.
Occasionally, we are even served in ways that dazzle us: everyone today seems to have stories about service reps who went
the extra mile. Products and services, too, have become freer of
defects and, to some extent, more customer friendly.

However, for the most part, these improvements may represent the low-hanging fruit, the things organizations were able
to do without significantly raising their costs, cutting into profits, or challenging basic goals or ways of working. Now that
this fruit has been picked, organizations interested in making
further progress face choices that, in an increasingly competitive and commoditized world, are becoming harder and
harder:

- The customer's need for quality and price versus the
  shareholder's need for profit.

- The customer's need for special attention versus the manager's need for productivity.

- The organization's need to appeal to more profitable customers versus its commitment to serve all customers.

- The customer's real need versus what the organization
  knows how—or is willing—to do.

Have these choices already become too difficult to deal
with? It sometimes seems that organizations today are awk-
wardly poised at the threshold of a new, tougher era of customer service for which they're not entirely sure they're
ready. The challenge they face is to find some way to reconcile these hard choices so that everyone comes out a winner:
the customers, the organization, the employees, and the
stockholders.

How Grassroots Leaders Let the Customer
Drive the Organization

We believe that the relatively few positive critical incidents in
our study may, in fact, be harbingers of the type of grassroots
leadership organizations will need to succeed in this tougher,
more competitive world. Such men and women will need to

act as visible and passionate advocates of the customer, acting out through their behaviors customer-related concepts and strategies—saying, in effect, "I'm making this effort because I think customers are so crucial to our success." In the process, they'll be helping customers emerge from the shadowy backstage corners of people's minds and take their place center stage as the true stars of the show.

When we analyzed the critical incidents to isolate the best practices successful grassroots leaders follow—those few critical areas in which they concentrate their efforts—we found three:

1. They take a stand for customers.

2. They model world-class customer service skills.

3. They are tireless in caring about customers.

According to our critical incidents, these best practices pack a much more powerful punch than customer service slogans or even customer data.

Grassroots Leaders Take a Stand for Customers

If you're going to become passionate about customers, you have to be prepared to raise the stakes. A group of incidents and interviews illustrates the conviction it takes to make changes that pay off for the customer, and often the courage required to advocate the customer's best interests. These incidents include removing barriers, balancing internal and customer needs, making all major decisions with the customer in mind, and tackling tough performance issues.

Judy Goetz, a sales trainer who also works on sales strategy at Fidelity and Deposit Company of Maryland, demonstrates the courage sometimes required to get the organization to make good on a professed customer commitment. Goetz was worried about a soon-to-be-released financial product she felt was poorly conceived and positioned. "We were putting something together to benefit us, not the customer," she said. "So in a sales training session I role-played a customer and asked, 'What's this going to do for me? Why should I buy something that's going to benefit you but not me?' Once the other people at the session thought it through, they realized they had to redesign the whole product." Goetz, who calls herself "just a training coordinator," couldn't support a product destined to fail because it ignored customer needs. Instead, she helped others see the product and, in a sense, themselves, from their customers' point of view.

A customer service rep in a software company stuck her neck out for the customer, even though it caused her team to miss a critical deadline. "She stood up for quality on her team, despite the schedule pressure to release the product," wrote the respondent. "Even when her manager was sloughing off [his own] quality responsibilities (a really poor leadership situation), she pushed the team to spend another day testing. [Later] she had the guts to say, 'Yes, it's over, but we have to ask what did we learn from this? If we don't take a look at it, it will probably happen again.'"

Anyone serious about letting the customer drive the organization will find the impact of her behavior on the other team members instructional. According to the respondent, "She alienated some people on the team, who are complacent and accept mediocrity. She energized others to find more quality-related activities to help the team move forward." It would be interesting to know the impact of her behavior on her manager, not to mention how much more productive the whole team might have been if he had demonstrated similar leadership himself.

Upgrade the Status of Customer Service within the Organization

In an incident at a university, a dean of students shocked his colleagues by treating students as if they were customers. Wrote the respondent, "The Dean of Students at our college took a proactive stance to student service issues. He used a series of instruments and focus groups to shape a quality customer service mentality in the college." Students as customers? One can only imagine the far-reaching impact of such a revolutionary mentality.

By raising the status of customer service, you are making the point that you consider it an important function of your operations. Jerry Carr, the president and CEO of Rochester Telephone, described his own efforts in this regard. "When you call our company with a complaint, you reach one of six experienced and empathic service reps. They used to work in our customer service group. Now they report directly to me." The implication is clear that they not only have the CEO's ear, they also have more leverage to get complaints resolved.

Des Byrne, managing director of Wavin Ireland, Ltd., an Irish company that makes plastic pipes, detached a very senior member of the management team and put him in charge of customer care. "People were surprised we had done that," he said in an interview, "because he was such a high resource. They hadn't realized customer care was so important." Byrne goes further in his elevation of the customer. "Even though we're basically a manufacturing company," he said, "I tell everyone we're 'market-driven and customer-focused.' I say Production is really there to serve Sales, because without Sales you wouldn't need Production, and you wouldn't need Distribution or Finance, either. For that matter, you wouldn't need me."

Don't Take No for an Answer

A group of field engineers felt strongly that their organization, a large U.S. transportation company, was ignoring customer complaints about the company's billing process, so they decided to take independent action. "They actually created surveys to gather customer data," said the respondent. "They used what they found out to help the finance team fix the process."

Balance Internal Needs and Customer Needs

The grassroots leaders' secret is to not get sucked into the apparent *either-or* nature of these needs, but to search instead for a *both-and* solution, which strikes a balance that works for everyone. "Our shipping clerk had his favorite truck carrier," said a manager at a Midwestern manufacturing company, "which was inexpensive but slow. Some customers complained, so the shipping clerk switched those customers to a faster, more reliable carrier which was also more expensive. But now the complaints from those accounts have stopped. In the long run, the cost trade-off was a good move."

One incident, also about shipping, underscores the impact of ignoring the customer when trying to keep costs down— and also the complex issues that affect the balance between customer and organizational needs. "The shipping clerk is totally focused on saving money," said the respondent, "and uses shipment methods that often don't get the product to customers in time. They then complain loudly." In this case the shipping clerk blames Manufacturing for not getting products ready to ship earlier, thereby forcing Shipping to go over its budget by engaging premium shippers. The message in this case, as in so many others: finding the right balance may require some cross-functional process improvements.

At an East Coast hospital a combination of factors, including new insurance limits and an increase in patients, required the hospital to strike a new balance between costs and care. As part of this restructuring, the maternity ward manager assigned one nurse to care for both mother and child, a departure from the previous practice of providing a different nurse for each. "Patients like it better and get better care," said the respondent, "and costs are more manageable. The big surprise is that staff like it. It creates a human connection between the nurse, the mother, the baby, the family, and the hospital."

Make Every Major Decision with the Customer in Mind

What you have to do to keep customers' welfare paramount isn't necessarily easy or obvious. In a negative example that makes this point, a well-meaning information technology director in a Canadian health care organization made some much-needed improvements in his own operation without getting input from hospital employees who had direct customer contact. "He reorganized his area without consulting us to get our support," said the respondent, a customer service provider, who said the IT improvements made it harder to serve customers. "The people making the decisions were only thinking of ways for things to work better for IT. They don't know enough about what *we* need to serve customers. Now, feelings of mistrust are rampant."

Take On Performance Issues

A number of critical incidents point out that leaders have to be willing to slog through some tough performance issues and, in extreme circumstances, to step in and set things right. "The supervisor saw significant lack of progress on a critical project for our primary customer," wrote a respondent from a Silicon Valley firm. "The individual was way too immersed in technical problems in the application software, with no useful output. The supervisor refocused the individual on the task at hand, identified ways to overcome the software deficiencies, provided a step-by-step plan for the whole project, and helped the individual decide how to start. With a plan, a goal, and a method to achieve it, this individual produced more in a week than in the previous month. The deadline was met and the customer was extremely satisfied."

Remove Barriers

A respondent described a barrier to customer service that was especially ironic, given the fact that she worked for a small independent phone company. When customers came into the office, the receptionist would determine the nature of their problem and then direct them to call the appropriate person from a phone on the opposite wall. Customers were not allowed to meet with the person face to face. "It was ironic," said the respondent. "Customers with problems serious enough to come to the office would stand in line, then be told use the phone!"

Grassroots Leaders Model World-Class Customer Service Skills

Nothing brings home how your organization esteems its customers more vividly than watching a formal or informal leader (and especially your manager) interact with a customer. Through what they say and do, successful grassroots leaders show that customers are highly valued and must be listened to.

Demonstrate through Your Behavior That Customers Should Be Heard and Valued

Successful grassroots leaders demonstrate through their skill, creativity, and total dedication that customers are of the utmost importance to them and, by implication, should be to everyone else in the organization as well. They show how to give customers what they ask for, but also what they might want but would never think to ask for. They are also able to demonstrate how to rebuild and even strengthen the relationship between an organization and an unhappy customer.

Unfortunately, however, many of the critical incidents were negative, for reasons of organizational or personal inadequacy, or a combination of the two:

- "He was simply reiterating company policies instead of listening and trying to help."

- "I was unable to provide insurance to a gentleman in a mobile home because we had nothing to offer him."

- "A customer wanted a travel kit sent out the same day. We couldn't do it."

- "The sales rep wouldn't exchange a broken phone that was still fairly new."

- "Our system is full of constraints. Extremely inflexible."

- "The rep actually laughed at the customer's confusion."

- "The agent left the customer on hold on and off for about thirty minutes."

- "The delivery people showed up three hours late for a scheduled appointment. They didn't have an explanation. And they didn't call the customer."

- "The representative said, 'Sorry, can't help you,' and basically hung up on the customer. She didn't offer any alternative."

Some incidents explicitly describe what happens when you narrowly apply rigid policies and procedures. Reported a respondent from a bank, "A customer wanted a refund for an overdraft charge. He wasn't claiming we'd made a mistake, but he said that since he was a long-term customer and it had only happened once, we should waive the charge. Bank policy states that loyalty and history cannot be a factor. So we refused, and he walked out. Later he called and closed his account."

Would you have the courage of the executive from the Bell operating company who regularly invited customers to say what they really thought of his organization? "To analyze and improve the many moments of truth that shape customer attitudes," the respondent wrote, "our manager invited customers to sit in on our strategy meetings and talk candidly about their experiences. We asked them to tell us about the good, the bad, and the ugly parts of getting their service installed. While they talked, we recorded their experiences on a chart. It was a revelation to learn how customers were really experiencing our organization."

In one incident a health insurance worker set an example of valuing customers by making a customer's needs her top priority despite some urgent deadlines of her own. "My customer was confused about some of his bills," she said. "He called me and asked for a face-to-face meeting to go over the paperwork—not something we normally do. He was insistent, though, so I told him to come in. I was extremely busy, but I put everything on hold and explained what was happening with his claims. The customer seemed very pleased."

Go Beyond the Expected

Going the extra mile impresses customers, and also sends a strong message within the organization about how important customers are. This message is evident in the example of what crew members at a Dallas gas and electric utility did to facilitate garbage pickup, which was by no means part of their regular work. The crew had torn up a street to install new gas lines. They left mounds of dirt and deep trenches everywhere, and had then moved on for a short while to another section. However, without prompting they returned on garbage pickup day and carried garbage cans from all the houses across the construction zone to an area where the truck could pick them up. After the pickup, they returned the cans to each house. The message they conveyed: Customers are important enough to devote extra thought and effort to.

In another incident an employee at a golf course mightily impressed some customers and also set a unique standard for other employees to follow. "Some customers wanted a tee time during a three-day weekend," said the respondent. "We were booked way in advance, so [this person] made several calls to competitor courses and finally booked a time. The customers were really appreciative and amazed we would do that. They'll do more business with us in the future."

Make the Most of a Bad Situation

When a product or service fails, leaving an angry customer in danger of defecting for good, successful leaders are able to turn this negative experience into a positive one for both customer and company. "I had some second thoughts about a favorite airline the night my flight was delayed," wrote one respondent about a travel experience. "It was a huge inconvenience, and I made that clear to the person at the gate. By the time I got home from the trip, there was a nice letter of apology waiting for me."

In another incident, a sales rep had to step in and clean up her supervisor's mess. "One of our reps was handling an upset customer who had previously spoken to the supervisor about a defective product he wanted to return," reported the respondent. "The supervisor had promised to take action, but she hadn't. So this rep bent our usual policy and helped the customer return the merchandise for credit. As a result, she managed to establish goodwill with a customer who had been very irritated."

In this and many similar incidents, successful leaders use an impromptu saving action, often called a recovery, to strengthen a customer relationship that's gone bad. Successful grassroots leaders recognize the customer's emotional state, take immediate steps to correct the error (for example, booking the customer on an immediate flight with another airline), and then follow up in some way (as in the case above, with a letter apologizing for the delay of the customer's flight).

In one incident a creative recovery eventually became standard procedure. During a power outage caused by a Midwestern snowstorm, an irate customer called the utility company to say he'd never be able to get to work on time without his electric alarm clock. A call center rep thoughtfully replied, "Go to bed. I'll call you in the morning." She did, much to the customer's delight. Today, it's common for that utility to offer wake-up calls during power outages.

Jerry Carr, Rochester Telephone's CEO, tells the story of a rep whose creative recovery saved a relationship with a customer who had been stood up for a telephone installation. "He had moved into a new residence, and was substantially inconvenienced that no one had shown up to install the phones," Carr said. "So the service rep went to our cellular department, rented a phone, and arranged to have calls to the customer's new home line forwarded to the cell phone. Then she jumped in her car, drove to the customer's residence, and delivered the phone, which he used at no charge until we got his service installed."

Grassroots Leaders Are Tireless in Caring about Customers

The leaders who successfully apply these practices are a little like dedicated and idealistic public defenders who always do their best for every client they represent. They have a genuine caring for customers that spurs them on to always do the best they can—both in direct customer interactions, and in those behind-the-scenes opportunities they find to make the organization more customer-friendly. This kind of dedication calls for a genuine caring that exceeds glib slogans or even specific skills. It appears to be based on a deeply held belief that customers are the organization's only reason for being. Whatever its source, it's more emotionally sustaining than the they-pay-our-bills-so-we've-got-to-be-nice-to-them attitude, with its hint of veiled resentment, or the-customer-is-always-right (so-we-must-be-wrong) point of view.

This tireless concern for customer welfare is evident in the story about a retired general manager of a Marriott hotel in the United Kingdom. It's told by Angie Risley, management development director with Whitbread PLC. "This person personally took ownership of service and customers," Angie said. "So then did everybody else. On all measures, including financial and customer measures, her results were better than for any of our other hotels.

"Her philosophy was, you look after your people and they will look after your guests. She personally walked around every area of the hotel. She ate lunch every day in the employee cafeteria. She greeted every employee by name. She held daily management meetings so everybody knew what was going on. She constantly sought customer feedback. When the surveys from guests were good, she posted them on the bulletin board. When they weren't, she immediately got people together to fix the problem. I would describe her as a person who was passionate about the business."

It's difficult to imagine how someone could maintain an unwavering focus on customers, day after day, without truly caring about their welfare—especially if doing so were not an explicit part of his or her job. It's one thing to respond to a customer in immediate distress, or even to take on the challenge of an irate customer. It's quite another to voluntarily speak up for the customer when the customer is a faceless abstraction, and when speaking up will almost certainly require greater effort, and quite possibly make other people angry.

To do what he did in the following incident, the design engineer in a Midwestern manufacturing plant must have cared a great deal about the customer. "We were under a deadline to manufacture a redesigned rack for one of our largest accounts," the respondent wrote. "The design engineer had completed his part of the project, but saw that Manufacturing did not have the parts on hand to assemble the new rack. Manufacturing seemed to be saying, 'Let somebody else worry about getting the parts down here.' So even though it was not his job, he expedited the parts from the supplier, picked them up in his own car, delivered them to Manufacturing, and worked side by side with them to get the new rack assembled and shipped on time."

Many of today's government employees are demonstrating real leadership when it comes to caring for customers. What's noteworthy about the following example—what suggests a deep reservoir of caring—are the lengths to which the person went for the customer, and her refusal to let obstacles stop her, even in the face of lackluster support from her supervisor. "Our agency is responsible for a national health survey," the clerk said. "I noticed that the initial response rate for households where Vietnamese was the primary language was dismal, which meant their health needs would be drastically underreported. I resolved to find a way to get the survey materials translated. My supervisor reluctantly agreed to let me do this, but only with a shoestring budget. I had to do extensive networking until I located a translator I could afford; I ended up finding one at my supermarket. She and her 16-year-old son did the translating. It was a work of art, but her typewriter didn't have a Vietnamese font, so I had to network again. I found a technician at a local software company who agreed to retype the document in the right font. We are now getting good responses from the Vietnamese households. Meeting them at their comfort level has contributed to our success."

In these critical incidents, successful grassroots leaders obviously care a great deal about their customers. But customers and their issues seldom crop up at opportune times: sometimes they demand attention when leaders are tired, or hopelessly overworked, or handling some *other* customer problem. What happens at such times? What happens when you dip into your emotional reservoir of caring and, deep though it may be, come up temporarily dry?

The answer is *emotional labor*,[1] a key component underlying almost all customer service transactions. Emotional labor is a leader's effort to express the emotions a customer consciously or unconsciously expects during a one-to-one interaction. Because customers are unpredictable, the leader may have to improvise, like an actor, to portray the expected emotions. In fact, among companies that see emotional labor as fundamental to customer loyalty, the Walt Disney organization explicitly uses the vocabulary of acting. Theme park employees are "cast members" who go "onstage" while on duty.

When there is a close match between what the customer expects and what the leader feels, emotional labor seems effortless, more like "being professional." However, when the leader does not actually feel the emotion a customer is looking for—genuine concern, for example, that the 50th customer to call during a heavy storm has lost power—that's when emotional labor really feels like labor. And the bigger the emotional gap, the more labor required to bridge it. For example, conducting focus groups to test out a new product concept may not feel very emotionally laborious. However, it's an altogether different emotional matter to take the results seriously enough to honestly question and even eliminate those aspects of the concept in which you have a heavy personal investment.

At times like these, people have the choice of either defending their position, or opening themselves up to what customers are telling them. Hearing what customers have to say under such circumstances can be difficult, requiring all the emotional labor you can muster to keep moving in a direction that will, if only in a small way, let the customer drive your organization.

Grassroots Leadership Step by Step

The following tools can help you build greater customer loyalty. These are located in the back of the book in "Tools: Grassroots Leadership Step by Step" (pages 144–154).

> **Cycle of Service Analysis (Tool 6).**   During an interaction with your organization, every customer moves through a series of events—for the customer, moments of truth—to achieve a given outcome. This tool helps you define that process, or cycle of service, and improve the customer's experience during each moment of truth (pages 144–146).

> **TACT Process (Tool 7).**   This tool helps you respond to some important issues shared by many of today's diverse customers—differences in language, physical abilities, comfort with technology, and culture. A simple process allows you to verify cues and respond tactfully and appropriately (pages 147–150).

> **Meeting Unspoken Customer Needs (Tool 8).**   Customers have needs beyond what they explicitly ask for. This

tool helps you identify and respond quickly and inexpensively to those needs. The payoff is an exceptional customer experience that reflects well on you and builds loyalty to your organization (pages 151–154).

 Although most organizations would probably say they are customer-oriented, the relatively few critical incidents for this strategy indicate that not enough people see work on behalf of the customer as a component of leadership. The competitive challenges in the years ahead suggest the need for memorable, emotion-involving leadership, which can breathe life into the abstract concept of *focusing on the customer.* The behaviors in the positive examples may indicate what such behavior needs to look like: visible and passionate advocacy in both direct customer contact and behind-the-scenes efforts to make the organization more customer-friendly. The best practices through which successful grassroots leaders make customers come alive are as follows:

1. They take a stand for customers.
2. They model world-class customer service skills.
3. They are tireless in caring about customers.

CHAPTER

Involve Every Mind

Fully 50% of all critical incidents fell under the four competencies that make up this strategy: "Support individual effort;" "Support team effort;" "Share information;" and "Make decisions that solve problems." Eighty percent of these incidents involved supervisory employees. About half the examples were negative.

ACCORDING TO OUR RESEARCH, LEADERS DON'T SIMPLY NEGLECT TO involve every mind; through their behavior they actively *uninvolve every mind,* often without knowing it. This behavior has serious consequences. In this day and age, no organization can prevail without a committed work force willing to contribute their best efforts to make sure the organization succeeds. The organization needs people who are willing to go the extra mile, work around roadblocks, and tap into their creativity ("good ideas are coming out," "the team is working on the change with a lot of commitment"). When it's neglected or performed badly, organizational problems are likely to persist or go underground ("this will only prolong the problem," "the organization lost, the employee has lost, and the work is still less than acceptable"). Strategic initiatives are likely to peter out, leaving the executive team to wonder what went wrong.

Uninvolved employees tend to feel underutilized, uninterested, and in many cases actively disinclined to contribute more than the bare minimum. The cartoon strip *Dilbert* (see Figure 4.1) graphically portrays employees who have been so mistreated that even the bare minimum is more than they feel like contributing. Scott Adams has created a world of outrageously bad leaders who do everything they can to offend and demotivate their employees—who still somehow manage to rise above the all-too-familiar frustrations, bureaucratic stupidities, and rude treatment.

Real life, however, isn't so funny. There is little that's more soul-destroying than having a job you don't care about or feel appreciated in. There is a tendency among some people to claim that, although they recognize the comic exaggerations in *Dilbert,* the attitudes it captures are endemic to organizational life and always will be. However, the findings that came out of our critical-incidents study paint an even darker picture. In this picture the difference between involved and uninvolved minds (or, as many of the incidents illustrate, actively *dis*involved minds) is the difference between organizational success and failure.

Figure 4.1 The cartoon strip *Dilbert.*

DILBERT© Distributed by United Feature Syndicate. Reprinted by Permission. BERRY'S WORLD© Distributed by United Feature Syndicate. Reprinted by Permission.

The people in our research see "involving every mind" as an extremely important part of a leader's job, and they don't think it's being done well. Here's the evidence:

- First, fully half of all the critical incidents in the study fall into the competencies that support this strategy: "support individual effort," "support team effort," "share information," and "make decisions that solve problems." Half of what people think it means to be a leader, in other words, has to do with "involving every mind."

- Second, half of these incidents were negative—instances in which leaders actively minimized individual and team effort; withheld information or missed opportunities to share it; and either sidestepped decisions that could have solved problems, or else arrived at decisions in a way that made things worse.

- Finally—and perhaps most disturbingly—a reading of these critical incidents indicates that the negative behaviors, which made a strong and even indelible impression on the respondents, were quickly forgotten by the people who performed them. Without knowing it, in other words, these leaders are poisoning the organization—the same organization they are responsible for maintaining and improving.

When People Don't Feel Involved

The following incidents suggest the flavor of the negative incidents. Although they all describe situations that might have come from a *Dilbert* cartoon, if you put yourself in the shoes of these people, you'll get a sense of just how unfunny and demoralizing the real-life impact on the individual—and by extension, on the organization—can be.

- "Our CEO interrupted our meeting by opening a closed door and with no comments or greeting told us to move someplace else because he needed the room. We consider the work of our team important. Our CEO let us know he doesn't."

- "Our manager called a meeting to set direction and roles and responsibilities. We waited for him for two hours. He finally called to say he'd have to reschedule, he was busy."

- "He called two workers into his office. He told one she wasn't doing well so he was going to move her to a new area . . . Then he told the other worker that he was promoting her into the first worker's old job. So in one meeting he managed to humiliate one person and make the other person feel very awkward and uncomfortable about her promotion."

- "He first heard about his grade-level promotion over e-mail when everybody else did."

- "When counseling his employees, he used vulgar and unbecoming language, and combined with a disrespectful tone of voice [he] basically destroyed the respect people had for him and his position."

- "She was out to gain some control and power in her new position. She belittled certain participants by announcing that their comments were inappropriate and would not be tolerated. She interrupted others and used angry language. The work environment became tense with mistrust and betrayal. Alliances are now forming against her."

Unfortunately, such examples of leaders behaving badly—exchanges in which they were seen as rude, inconsiderate, blatantly insensitive, and even vulgar—were not uncommon. Granted, they don't tell both sides of the story. Maybe the leaders were trying to regain control of a chaotic situation. Maybe they were so busy and under so much pressure that they either lost control of themselves, or else felt somehow justified in not making more of an effort to behave better. What's important here, however, is how their behavior was perceived by those on the receiving end: none of these people saw any justification for it. As far as the respondents were concerned, these leaders had dug themselves into a deep hole and were going to have a very hard time climbing out of it. Their leadership had inspired not greatness, but disgust.

Does any of this resonate with your own experience as either the receiver or the perpetrator? If you've experienced this kind of gross behavior from a leader, you no doubt know the anger and frustration it can generate. If the behavior was more subtle—a sarcastic comment about your abilities, perhaps, or a failure to recognize a special effort on your part— you may have brushed it off or, in fact, never have noticed what did or didn't happen. Still, even if you didn't feel like going ballistic, the leader's actions certainly didn't deepen your commitment to your work.

In terms of your own leadership behavior, you're probably doing what we, the authors of this book, did when we first read these incidents, which was to cast around for times when we might have been guilty of demotivating, or even offending, people. The critical incidents make it painfully clear how easy it is to be the unwitting villain in a work situation.

In terms of determining the level of commitment in your organization, you might ask yourself the following questions:

- Do strategic initiatives start off strong but never produce results?

- Does your organization, despite its claims, actually support the risk-taking necessary to encourage new ideas?

- Which does your organization value more highly, the ability to spot mistakes or the ability to make things happen?

- What about your own state of mind? Do you feel a commitment to your job? Do you feel recognized and valued for your efforts?

How Grassroots Leaders Involve Every Mind

What's ironic about this negative state of affairs is that it's easy to fix. It's not a question of expensive motivational programs or complicated planning infrastructures. In fact, when we looked at where the successful leaders in our study concentrate their efforts, we found that what they do is very basic:

1. They listen.
2. They share information.
3. They coach.

4. They praise.

5. They are patient, yet persistent.

It turns out Mom was right. If you're polite and helpful, share, pay attention, and always find something positive to say, you'll be successful not only on the playground but also on the job. What's more, it seems almost impossible to overdo these behaviors. The more leaders listen, for example, or the more they praise, the more commitment they create.

Successful leaders seem to have completely integrated these Leadership 101 competencies into how they do their work. Like professional tennis players, they have mastered the basics so well that they are free to concentrate on the more complex strategic question of how to win. Without the basics, however, strategizing can't pay off. You may see the perfect opportunity for a crosscourt backhand, but if you can't hit one, your insight is wasted.

Grassroots Leaders Listen

One of the biggest lessons in these critical incidents is how much people appreciate leaders who hear them out. Successful leaders don't listen to ferret out people's errors, or to spy, or to gather evidence to support their own preconceived ideas. They listen instead to learn, to get results, to identify good ideas, and to help others do well. Because they listen they have more information, and so are better equipped to be better leaders. Now more than ever, knowledge is power. According to Monica Gleeson, Personnel Manager at Sigma Wireless Communications in Dublin, "The most effective leaders listen to the words and to the words between and behind the words. They pay attention to tone of voice and body language, to what's not said, as well as what is. Leaders who don't do this are only half-listeners."

When leaders don't take the time to listen, the impact on employee commitment can be costly. During a major restructuring, an Australian-based account executive for an international sales organization made repeated phone appointments with her boss in England to discuss some steps she thought needed to take place. However, although she was one of the top performers in the company, her boss was never at his phone at the appointed time. "I've always felt like a business partner," she reported, "but considering my boss's lack of response, I now feel more like just an employee." Her level of commitment, in other words, has gone way down.

Many times there are real pressures—shortness of time, cost, urgency—that seem to leave no room for listening. In such cases it might help to keep the following payoff in mind: "She kept cool under pressure; explored options to the problem; allowed individuals to air their concerns; kept the discussion focused and on track; put herself in others' shoes; made a difficult decision after all input was received. She gained credibility; others followed through and supported the decision."

Time and again, the critical incidents underscore the value of making the effort to listen: "When presented with a dilemma regarding a course of action, [he] demonstrated effective leadership by asking these people who would be directly affected by the action to provide opinions. He guided us through the different options, identifying the best- and worst-case outcomes."

Listen to Build Support and Consensus

When leaders operate from the assumption that other people have ideas worth listening to, not only do good ideas emerge, but so does a willingness to support them. This incident makes the point: "He listened to the concerns and comments being expressed and took them seriously, avoiding 'company line' answers," wrote one respondent. "[He was obviously] committed to taking action. I felt heard and valued by his behavior and therefore was more willing to work with him."

In some situations it's possible to use listening to develop a personal support network. That's what a senior human resources manager did when she grew frustrated in her efforts to get the plant manager to approve a course of action she felt was vital to employees. According to one of her staff members, "[The manager] gathered her staff and asked for help and ideas. [We] worked through a process and together delivered a plan and strategy to influence the general manager and show him the benefits to the employees, the plant, and to him. She said getting others involved helped share the pain. It led to a better plan [which] the plant manager ultimately accepted."

Leaders can also use listening to help build consensus and team feeling among people who need to work together. One leader who needed to develop a strategy for his department used a combination of one-on-one and group meetings to gather opinions. In the individual sessions, employees got to voice personal concerns, which they might not have raised during a group meeting. "Then he called a meeting for everyone to hear all the ideas and thoughts, to formulate a strategy, and to get buy-in," the respondent wrote. Having been heard in the one-on-one sessions, everyone was able to concentrate on the strategy at the group meeting: "The employees felt genuine support of a unified strategy. The proposal was presented to higher-level management, thus providing the employees with a sense of contribution as well as having their case heard."

Listen to Resolve Disputes

This is an area in which successful leaders do a lot more listening than talking. Referring to a program developer who was in charge of a project that got off-track, one person wrote, "He asked for our side of the story before coming to any conclusions. Then, when he decided, he gave very good, specific feedback about our activities: what he liked and what he didn't like. His willingness to listen made me feel better about taking risks, and knowing he didn't go crazy when we did something wrong makes it easier to recover from mistakes."

When someone wades in without getting the full picture, people may feel betrayed and outraged; these are not emotions that enhance commitment. "Someone falsely accused an employee of failing to do something," wrote one person. "The manager didn't get the full information, listened only to one side of the story, and did not approach anyone else in the department to find out what may have happened. He ripped apart this employee [and] upset the other people in the department, because [the person who made the accusation] was lying through his teeth."

Listen to Facilitate

You don't have to be a manager to find opportunities in which listening will produce dividends. In one critical incident two teams needed to start working together. At their first joint meeting, the one person who happened to be a member of both teams took it upon herself to make sure everyone had a chance to speak and say what was on his or her mind. "In conversations with some of the participants after the meeting," wrote another team member, "it was agreed the meeting was successful and both teams had a chance to bring up their important issues. The teams have a better understanding . . . of where the other is coming from. The . . . meeting was a prelude to an all-day session in which resolution of the issues will be worked on. The meeting was important in getting the issues on the table, so we know what needs to be worked on."

Grassroots Leaders Share Information

Although it seems self-evident that information should flow freely within organizations, many of the critical incidents were about information being withheld. Respondents felt discounted when they weren't given the information they needed, and often made an explicit connection between a lack of information and a lack of progress. They also made various assumptions about why leaders were denying them information, none of which they liked or thought necessary:

> **To keep them calm.**   People often think that leaders withhold information for fear they'll "make the natives restless," and they resent the implied lack of trust. "My company is currently navigating a reorganization," wrote one respondent about another person who pushed for more information, "and the corporate big dogs were leaning toward making the official announcement after the fact. This person successfully convinced them that

keeping employees informed as the process moved along was a better idea. I have no proof, but would strongly suggest that his efforts significantly reduced rumor mill productivity and kept the anxiety level lower than it would have been, not to mention the mood of the troops was better."

To move faster.   Trying to keep decisions secret, even with the best intentions, can backfire. In one incident, a senior manager changed the work assignments of several people without talking either to the staff involved or to their supervisor. "The staff was upset," the person wrote. "The supervisor could not answer their questions, and not much work got done. Approximately ten other people who were not involved got dragged into listening to their coworkers complain and express their frustration." The senior manager apparently thought by not telling anybody what he was doing he could move faster, but in the final analysis the opposite was true.

To keep information out of the "wrong hands." Although some information should be distributed on a need-to-know basis, in today's organization it's not always easy to figure out who needs to know what. Joan, an operations manager for a publishing firm, starts with the assumption that everyone might need to know everything. She evaluates almost every piece of information that crosses her desk—memos, articles, e-mails—in terms of who else might possibly need it, and sends it on. "They can always throw it away," she said, "but maybe they can use it. Or maybe they think they can't, but six months down the road something comes up and they'll make the link."

To hide their own ignorance.   The message to all those leaders who resist discussing issues that are still unresolved or for which they don't have all the answers: people appreciate being included and admire leaders big enough to admit they don't know everything. Wrote one person: "This leader was addressing a group of employees. Employees were feeling insecure because of a rapid change [and they] wanted to know answers. The answers were not available. [However,] this leader was able to explain processes, hurdles, and expected timelines, always clarifying that things are changing."

If you're in doubt about whether to share information, you might want to remember that not one of the critical incidents praised anyone for withholding information. On the contrary, they illustrate the advantages leaders achieve when they are open and straightforward.

Unearth Concerns and Resistance

Time and again, critical incidents underscored the fact that people respond to leaders who are willing to stand up and take the heat, so to speak; and that in the course of such open discussions, many concerns and negative feelings get resolved. One leader received high marks for her openness and courage: "She brought together groups that had some problems in the past and led them through team-building exercises. She wasn't afraid to face negativity. The team members felt more comfortable with each other; a new level of respect was reached between the team members and the leader."

There's no reason you have to be a manager to get a dialogue going. During a training class in which many participants were being very negative about a new company program, one frontline employee spoke up and expressed his support for it, and gave his reasons, encouraging others to start talking. In the ensuing discussion, "many participants who [were] . . . 'on the fence' saw his side and, while not everyone 'bought in,' many became more open-minded." In cases like this, one person's positive comments may not turn the tide. However, if he hadn't said anything, the others would never have been prompted to reevaluate their negative views.

People appreciate grassroots leaders who are willing to discuss the bad news as well as the good. In one post-downsizing incident, the supervisor called a meeting of his newly reduced staff to discuss how the work should get done. "Everyone's ideas were solicited," one staff member wrote, "and after articulating some of the group's boundaries, the supervisor allowed us to give input and share in decision-making. This meeting cleared the air at a time when the disintegrating role of the group was leading to poor communications, individualistic behavior, and a loss of trust."

Or as Janet Clement, an internal consultant with the U.S. Mint, put it, "When leaders give answers and don't skirt it, you feel more connected to the meat and grind of the organization."

We know that people remember information better if it is presented in story form, especially when there is a personal element. In one critical incident, a boss dropped in on a team-building session and told some stories about his own problems with teams. The respondent said, "He modeled being open, and this encouraged the group to begin sharing their own stories. It helped create a team feeling and made us appreciate the boss."

Don't Micromanage

There can be a fine line between sharing information and telling people what to do. In the critical incidents people express deep appreciation for not being micromanaged. "She provided the direction and the boundaries," one person said, "and let me determine my objectives." Said another: "He is aware of areas of expertise of each staff member under his direction. When a problem or issue arises, he briefs us fully, gives clear direction and assigns the project to the appropriate staff member, and trusts him/her to take appropriate action without micromanaging the project. By keeping other staff members informed, they can contribute important information from different perspectives."

Grassroots Leaders Coach

Many people see coaching as the skill that most clearly separates the inspiring from the workaday leader, perhaps because there seem to be so many challenging dimensions to coaching: how to initiate it; when and how much to get involved; when to back off; what to say, and what to leave unsaid; and how best to follow up. The successful leaders in our study understood how to straddle that fine line between too little and too much coaching, and to apply this understanding in all kinds of contexts: with individuals in their work groups, with their bosses, and with teams.

If we were to identify the one critical incident that best embodies what might be called inspired coaching, it would probably be the following story. It was told by someone who came to his manager with a proposal for a plan of action, which the manager had real questions about: "My manager was honest in expressing his concerns, but he had confidence in my intelligence and abilities, so he supported my decision despite his doubts. When asked, he offered ideas but did not force me to follow his line of thinking. As a result, I confidently pursued my own course of action, was successful, and made us both look good. Had I failed, I would have learned from it without fear of being penalized."

This incident has the elements that we'd all like in a coach but too seldom get: straight talk, but no restrictions; more suggestions than direct orders; a willingness to go out on a limb to support our efforts; and above all, the knowledge that we will always have a safe haven to return to, even if we mess up.

This approach received praise in another critical incident: "[She] used open communication with her group in asking for suggestions and/or comments in order to initiate a new project. In effect, [she handed] over the actual process to the team/staff in a democratic fashion without losing jurisdiction over it. The team will have ownership. [The manager's] staff is made an integral part of the project, and enhances team effort."

Don't Be Afraid to Let Go

If people have been given responsibility for an assignment, they don't like leaders who then give orders under the guise of coaching. This was the case for someone who was asked by his manager to organize part of a huge presentation the manager was closely identified with throughout the organization. "He asked me to organize the presentation," the person stated, "and then outlined not only the purpose of the presentation, but also the details of how it was to be done, the details to be covered, and even sketched out the overheads to be used. I was left to just do the work in task fashion. My thoughts and ideas were not acceptable. . . . I was not trusted to contribute my ideas."

Another person described a similar situation, underlining the negative impact of the leader's behavior: "He made all the decisions ahead of time. . . . [At one of our meetings he] asked if we had other ideas. If we did, he shot them down. . . . He seemed inflexible and took everything personally. Everyone clammed up. We all said very little after that. People didn't look to him for guidance or control."

It's evident from such stories that when leaders are unable to completely let go of a high-stakes assignment, the results they're so concerned about may suffer, as in this example: "He told us what needed to be done, how it needed to be done, and never explained why or gave us any latitude to make our own decisions. We didn't put our whole hearts in the project and as a result, it was a medium job." Ironically, it was precisely this manager's attempt to guarantee a good outcome that produced a mediocre one instead.

On the other hand, when you've laid the groundwork so you can truly let go, the results can be extraordinary. Gary Kral, training specialist at Cessna Aircraft, had such a leader. He gave Gary a big assignment during a staff meeting, and then went off to Canada for two weeks. "'This project is yours,' was the last thing he told me," Gary remembers. "In the next two weeks I had to commit to over $85,000 in expenditures on my hand-shake alone. I knew I wasn't specifically authorized, but I'd worked with Fred for a number of years and I was keyed into his vision and values, so I knew what kind of actions were appropriate and which were not. The project was successful and I actually got a big promotion out of it."

Coach Sideways

You don't need to be a manager to be a coach. In fact, you may have more insight as a peer than a manager. In the following incident, a member of a work team who was feeling negative about the team's efforts went to another member to resolve her doubts. "She counseled me," the person wrote. "She shared her observations and suggested what I could do to turn our whole department back on the right track. She discussed our value system and got me focused on our mission. I became a positive, enthusiastic team member who influenced others to become productive again."

People are often reluctant to coach a peer for fear of butting in or looking like a know-it-all. Done effectively, however, peer coaching presents a perspective not available from any other source. In the following incident, a supervisor went to a peer for help in dealing with another department. "[He] listened to my concerns about a confrontation I had had [with people from another department] . . . He shared [with me] some of the pressures that were affecting that department, and we talked potential long-term solutions. He never told me what to do. A day later he talked with this department, but did not disclose anything [we had] said. . . . He was totally professional and respected decisions I made. This resulted in my receiving an apology [from the department] . . . More importantly, it led to a candid, open discussion on relationships between departments, perceptions that drive decisions, and how we can improve the situation."

Coach Up

Managers frequently complain that they don't get enough feedback on their performance from their direct reports or others. In the following incident, someone who received an e-mail from a manager containing inappropriate remarks about other people discussed the situation with that manager. She focused her comments on the company's stated principles of maintaining every person's self-esteem and supporting constructive relationships among people. According to the respondent, this woman "noted how [the manager's] behavior was not in accordance with . . . [these] principles, while personally demonstrating their use in this real case. (The meeting was private.) The senior person no longer . . . writes inappropriate e-mail. His public behavior is also better."

Coach Teams to Come Up with Their Own Solutions

In one of the critical incidents a team came to a manager for help with a problem they were having. In describing the manager's response, one member said: "She included the entire staff in the decision making process. She . . . helped us to focus our problem-solving attention in the right direction. We were provided with the needed support and information yet we were also given the freedom to run with our solution. The problem was taken care of in an efficient and timely manner. The decision was well-accepted because it was based on the needs/concerns of all involved people. The staff felt a sense of pride and accomplishment."

Coach to Develop Future Team Muscle

One critical incident highlights the need to help teams develop extra capabilities they may need to deal with problems down the road. For example, faced with the possibility that the work group might lose a member, the manager of one team encouraged the team to strategize ways to handle their workload with fewer people. The team appreciated the manager's foresight. "We spent time on examining and prioritizing and redistributing the work," wrote a team member, "contacting our internal clients to see what was important to them. At this stage, it was 'disaster planning.' We didn't specify which of us would be missing, but kept it a flexible situation. When we were actually faced with the situation, we had already gone through the venting process and were able to make use of the work we had done earlier. We were therefore able to accommodate this challenge in a positive way."

Coach Teams to Monitor Their Workload

Teams, just like individuals, can sometimes become overloaded with work without knowing it, and not know to ask for help. In the following critical incident, a manager helped his team come to the realization that they needed to do some rearranging. "He took his department to lunch. [They] reviewed all the projects they had to do . . . [and] realized that the department was overwhelmed with too many important short-term projects with heavy due dates. He authorized a temporary clerical person to cover phones [so that] the department could 'shut down,' go to a meeting room and do concentrated work on the projects . . . The work effort appeared to go from 'overwhelmed' fire-fighting to a concentrated and focused work place."

Coach to Improve the Lives of Team Members

Although people resented coaching that was too directive, they also objected to the leader who sidestepped a coaching challenge, especially when the quality of their work life was at stake. In one example, a team was preparing for ISO 9000 certification, and felt its project manager was much too volatile and needed some coaching from her manager. "The project manager for this certification . . . has strong organizational skills but under stress, she can be brutal in her interactions," said a member of the team. "Her boss was specifically challenged to give her candid feedback on these behavioral issues [but he] side-stepped the issue, reviewing only the results and ignoring the behaviors. There was no ownership on his part to give her important, career-impacting feedback. This failure to give candid feedback is flagrantly poor leadership. How can the team member be expected to improve if they don't get told there's a problem? How can the standards for respectful interactions be kept intact when people are allowed to behave in abusive ways? The ISO project will end this summer when we are certified. There is no department willing to take on this volatile person (who thinks she's doing fine!). What a shame."

In another incident, the unit manager's behavior was having a destructive impact on a team, but the team's leader did nothing, "[even though he] recognized the cause of the problem was the unit manager . . . [He] did not give advice or coaching to the unit manager even though he was in a role to do so. Instead, he allowed the team to flounder; did not give direction in terms of expectations; did not take initiative to improve a poor situation. [The leader was] non-decisive . . . The team members continued with their problems and [as a result their leader] is perceived as weak or afraid of speaking the truth."

Grassroots Leaders Praise

If these critical incidents are any indication, you'll never involve every mind as effectively with criticism, no matter how constructive, as you will with praise. Criticism makes people defensive, which makes it harder for them to hear. In every single incident about receiving positive recognition, people talk about how it boosted their energy and made them feel like doing more. Many spoke of the fond memories of recognition they had been given, memories that kept them going during difficult times.

On the other hand, people referred negatively to leaders who didn't praise any behavior short of the miraculous, or who thought one piece of praise a year was more than enough.

A close reading of the critical incidents supports the belief that leaders dramatically underuse recognition, and raises the question of why this should be true. Giving praise seems to raise a lot of red flags. Will people come across as insincere? Manipulative? Can they do it gracefully? Will too much praise spoil people? Create pressure for pay increases? Are there cultural dimensions to how much praise is appropriate?

One reason may be the difficulty some people have in accepting praise; their discomfort can embarrass the praise-giver as well. The critical incidents make it clear, however, that despite what they may say ("Oh, it was nothing") people love to be praised. Although no one appreciates being manipulated through a series of empty compliments, if done right, praise is very hard to overdo. The secret is to become a keen observer of the good as well as the bad, keep the praise focused on very specific behaviors, and always frame it in the context of how this behavior helps you or others do their work better.

Your timing is also important. The closer to the behavior, the more effective the recognition, so don't hesitate for fear you won't do it right, or wait for the perfect moment to come along. If you wait too long, the other person may be so angry you'll have to apologize for your own behavior before you can praise his or hers. For example, someone in a critical incident described how he served as temporary human resources manager at a facility 1,000 miles away from corporate headquarters. During his nine months in this job he implemented many changes, and eventually was promoted for his efforts. What stuck in his craw was the lack of response from the corporate VP of human resources at headquarters, with whom he had a dotted-line reporting relationship. Even though he knew this person was not demonstrative, he still expected some kind of appreciation from him. "It took almost two weeks for this individual to acknowledge I had returned, thank me for a job well done and congratulate me on my promotion. [It made me feel] like I really didn't count in this organization. I wondered why I had just spent nine months living out of a suitcase if it couldn't even be acknowledged. I was disappointed, hurt and angry even though everybody knows this person 'is just like that.' "

People appreciate being recognized for their efforts, whether they've yet produced massive results. You don't need to wait for monumental achievements or the completion of the project. The following incidents cover a wide range of behaviors. In most cases, the impact on the receiver far outweighs the effort required of the giver. In other words, when you praise you get a sizable return on your investment.

- "In a short three-minute message, our CEO thanked 1,000 employees, gave us new information and shot down the rumor mill about the company being sold. The message made us feel important. A simple thank-you can go a long way."

- "[A leader] wrote a memo recognizing positive results resulting from extensive team work during a situation when tensions were high and elements (weather) uncooperative. Morale has been at a lull for many, many months, if not years, but [the memo] has done something positive to the basic attitudes of most employees for now."

- "The day we finally got [the 1099 and W-2] forms in the mail, our supervisor brought in ice cream cones, nuts, and chocolate sauce, and we were all encouraged to take a break together and heave a sigh of relief. The ice cream and group break helped ease the tension of the week and brought everyone together to know how much he appreciated all of our work."

Know That When You Recognize One, You Impact Many

When you give someone recognition in public, you exert an impact far beyond that person, as the following team member reported. "We have a very shy person on our team," she said.

"In a meeting while everyone else was describing their accomplishments for the week, she was silent. Our team leader reminded her of the great idea she had come up with for training the warehouse personnel. She smiled and blushed a little—she seemed very pleased that her efforts had been noticed. It was good for all of us to hear what she had done for the company. [Hearing him give her public credit] made us all feel that this is a good place to work."

When you recognize someone's behavior, you let everyone know the kind of behavior you think is worth recognizing. "I worked on a document which will be used as a handout to the public," wrote a desktop publisher. "I was able to produce a good-looking and informative flyer in a short period of time. My manager and his manager both complimented me on the work I did, and told me how helpful it would be in their upcoming public meeting. I was motivated to do at least as good a job next time, and felt that I could probably succeed again because I now had a clear understanding of their standards."

Gain Credit for Yourself by Giving It Away

This paradox was illustrated in the following incident: "The board of directors asked a department manager to make a presentation about an innovative program which is receiving very favorable comments. The department manager brought along the supervisor who conceived and implemented the [program]. They jointly addressed the board, with the department manager commending his supervisor in front of the board. The department manager has won the loyalty of his supervisor, probably for life. The board respects the department manager for his honesty—giving credit where credit is due and sharing the glory. Other supervisors of his will likely attempt innovations, since they know they will be recognized."

Grassroots Leaders Are Patient, Yet Persistent

For every critical incident in which someone appreciates having the time to go over details, voice concerns, or learn from mistakes, there's probably a leader on the other side of the interaction who is making a conscious effort to be patient. As one leader said in an interview, "There are times when it's all I can do not to say 'just do it, for heaven's sake,' or 'do it this way,' or 'why are you being so negative?' Frankly, it can be exhausting."

Involve every mind is accomplished by invitation, not by directive, and people may not accept invitations when they're first offered. They may actively turn them down, again and again. They may throw up objections and roadblocks that make you wonder why you ever made the effort to involve them in the first place.

Faced with resistance, successful leaders offer no ultimatums and close no doors. Instead, they try to keep the momentum going. They keep listening, sharing information, coaching, and praising, and trust that in time people will accept their invitation.

Grassroots Leadership Step by Step

The tools described hereafter can be found in "Tools: Grassroots Leadership Step by Step" (pages 155–167).

Proactive Listening (Tool 9).   This tool provides a series of specific steps for improving your listening habits and managing and focusing conversations. The techniques are especially helpful when you have to deal with complex and emotionally charged issues, and when you are dealing with people whose ways of relating to others is different from yours (pages 155–159).

Coaching: Bringing Out the Best in Others (Tool 10). This tool helps you to recognize diverse coaching opportunities, plan a coaching session, and offer your coaching advice in a way that doesn't sound as if you're giving orders. You can use this step-by-step approach with people on your own team as well as with people in other groups or functions (pages 160–163).

Giving Recognition (Tool 11).   This tool helps you to identify behaviors you want to reinforce, and provides a series of steps you can take when giving recognition to make sure the exchange feels comfortable and achieves its intended impact (pages 164–167).

Organizations can't survive without the active commitment of the entire workforce. *Involving every mind* is seen by people in the critical incidents as a huge component of leadership, yet half of all the incidents they described were negative, with behaviors ranging from thoughtless to rude and even vulgar. Although the impact of this behavior was long-term and extremely damaging, the clear implication was that few of the leaders were aware of what they had done. What emerges from the positive incidents is that successful leaders concentrate their efforts on what might be called the basics of leadership:

1. They listen.
2. They share information.
3. They coach.
4. They praise.
5. They are patient, yet persistent.

CHAPTER

Manage Work Horizontally

The critical incidents for this strategy (17% of the total) were "Manage cross-functional processes;" "Display technical skills;" "Manage projects;" and "Manage time and resources." These incidents are the most evenly balanced between examples of managers and nonmanagers.

THIS STRATEGY RECOGNIZES THAT WHEN IT COMES TO SUBSTANTIALLY boosting an organization's performance (1) improving the way departments work together is where the greatest leverage lies, and (2) there's probably no leadership task today that's more frustrating. When you manage work horizontally, you're dealing with what are variously known as cross-functional issues, or breakdowns in handoffs between departments. These are the uncharted white spaces on the organization chart in which sharks, whirlpools, and fierce crosscurrents threaten anyone brave enough to sail into this territory. It's a world in which you seldom have the clear-cut authority you want, or control over the resources you need. To be successful, you need to keep looking sideways and behind you, even as you fix your eyes firmly on the goal ahead—because in today's less hierarchical, more project-oriented, outcomes-driven world, just because someone up the food chain issues an order doesn't mean it's necessarily going to be carried out.

● ● ●

Don sat at his desk with one hand on the phone, thinking about his product development team meeting coming up that afternoon and wondering just what had happened to the food chain at his recently merged publishing company. This was the meeting at which his team was supposed to sign off on the development plan they'd all spent the last three months working on. Don seriously doubted they would do so.

The team had been formed—or so he thought at the time—to replace a popular but aging series of travel guides called *Go Away!* Going into the assignment, he'd been excited. He'd made a special effort to get a representative sample of the key stakeholders from both companies on the team. Included were marketing, sales, and support people from across the merged organization, with the majority coming from the company that had originally published the series. Don and two other editors came from the other company in the merger.

Now, sitting at his desk, Don found it hard to admit that the project had stalled out, but what else could he think? Somehow everything he had tried to do had violated an unspoken rule of one company or the other—starting with the initial focus groups he had wanted to conduct. The editors in Don's former company had always worked as closely as possible with bookstore buyers, book clubs, and readers throughout all phases of planning and development—getting their initial ideas, and then testing and retesting concepts and materials until they had something that tested well in the marketplace. Apparently, however, team members from the other company felt more comfortable with an author-based approach. Though they'd never said it in so many words, Don had heard that they thought too much market involvement, especially in the initial stages, diluted the authors' expertise and resulted in a fragmented, superficial product.

He hated to bring his boss into the problem, but Don's discouragement was almost complete. He felt like he was walking on eggs, never knowing when he might inadvertently offend somebody or break some sacred corporate rule. By this point, team members had begun to skip meetings; their managers seemed to have "other priorities" for them. Somehow, Don had talked most of them into attending today's meeting, but if they didn't sign off on the plan, how could they ever move into the development phase? How would they meet their publication date?

Don sighed, and with a great deal of reluctance he picked up the phone to call his boss, Leonard.

•   •   •

Managing work horizontally is based on the understanding that even though organizations are set up in vertical departments, the actual flow of work is horizontal across departments. In today's organizations, this understanding has led to all the cross-functional projects and teams set up to eliminate entrenched inefficiencies that live in the undefined "white spaces" between departments and work groups. In fact, many of the critical incidents in our research cite the dramatic improvements that often occur when organizations first take this horizontal approach. This was the case for the manager of a purchasing department, which interacted with almost every other part of the organization. "The purchasing department manager identified the most labor-intensive processes and automated them," the respondent said. "This reduced the time it took to complete these tasks by 60 percent." Similar results were realized by a corporate controller who moved the financial files from all departments onto one hard drive. In the words of the respondent, "Now they are accessible to all individuals. We can now process information much faster."

Of all the critical incidents in our research, those that define this strategy are most likely to include references to concrete improvements, along with examples of leaders making other people's jobs specifically easier or harder, especially regarding the issue of saving time. Respondents were impressed when leaders were able to foster cooperation between departments traditionally at odds with each other, as in this manufacturing example: "A new maintenance manager was able to redefine roles on the shop floor. He [worked with the machine operators] to change the orientation from 'breakdown-crisis response' to one where everyone took a planned, predictive-care approach. . . . We have seen the results: reliability rates are improving and maintenance costs are going down. In addition the staff has a visibly improved sense of pride and a feeling of control over their fate."

The central figures in the critical incidents for this strategy are just as likely to be individual contributors as managers or supervisors: "The vice president's secretary did the right things right, cut out steps, combined documents [coming in from various work groups] and substantially shortened the process for distributing monthly operational reports." Or, in another case: "The public relations assistant convinced us to use a mailing house to get material out to remote locations. This change cut our mailing costs in half."

At Rochester Telephone an administrative assistant found a way to save photocopying time both for those making copies, and for those in accounting who had to assign photocopying costs to the proper departments each month. Instead of each department counting its copies through the use of an Auditron (a counting device that plugs into the copiers), why not simply apportion the monthly photocopy charges according to a fixed formula based on the number of people in each department? "We probably save $80,000 a year in accounting costs alone," said the respondent, "not to mention the time saved because you don't have to go back for your department's clicker which we were always forgetting."

The critical incidents stress the positive impact leaders have when they pay attention to the human concerns that arise during work redesign and process improvement. A director of nursing at a hospital was praised for using her awareness of these concerns to keep the project on schedule. "She had the task of leading a cross-functional team in redesigning the role of nursing assistants so they could take on more varied duties," the respondent said. "The project was deemed controversial by the staff to begin with; however, this nursing director successfully brought together a task force that spanned six departments. She took great care in launching the task force. As a result, territorial issues were seldom raised; people said they really felt like they were working toward a common goal. The team didn't waste time or repeatedly go back to issues as to how decisions were made. They made quick progress."

Leaders who are successful with this strategy seem to take a systems-oriented view of everything, not just work. One respondent reported on a volunteer's process improvement efforts at her church. She wrote, "He figured out we could shorten the time it takes to count the Sunday collection from two hours to one hour if we just counted the money once after the twelve o'clock service, instead of twice. This makes the volunteers happy." (If this weren't a church, one might be tempted to ask if such an improvement would also make auditors happy.)

When Work Isn't Managed Horizontally

When this strategy is not performed well, respondents describe the impact primarily in terms of increased frustration and more work: "nothing ever got resolved," "made more work for the other representatives," and "wasted time and effort in some areas; [created] frustration and resentment on the part of some employees."

•   •   •

Don's conversation with his boss had been frustrating. Don had been looking to Leonard for some help and support before the meeting, but Leonard had been maddenly balanced. His even-handedness was beginning to drive Don crazy. Don was looking for an advocate.

"The travel series is their former company's product," Leonard had said. "It's their baby. How would we like it if someone started messing around with one of *our* products?"

"I know!" Don replied. "But the fact is, the decision was made to replace *Go Away!,* wasn't it? Doesn't Sandra know that? I mean, otherwise why did they set up this product development team? And what about the recommendations of the sales force? Everybody thinks the series is just too old!!"

"Right," Leonard replied, in his I-hear-what-you're-saying-but-I'm-not-necessarily-agreeing-with-you tone.

"What do you mean, right?! Right *what?!*" Don sensed himself dangerously close to the edge. "Why can't anybody around here make a decision that sticks?! Whose decision is it, anyway?"

"With this merger we've become a new organization," Leonard said. "Nobody knows what the rules are. We're all having problems like these. I know I am."

"I expected people would need to get into every little detail at first," Don said. "But once they decided we were on the right path, I figured they'd relax. That's what always happens. Except this time."

"We've got a lot of responsibilities to sort out. I know it's frustrating, but I don't think ordering people to do this is the best way to go."

"So what are you saying?"

"What I'm saying," Leonard said, "is that I'd like to see you and Sandra find some way to work things out at your level. I'm not saying it's easy, but believe me, in the long run it will be in your best interests to do it that way."

That conversation had occurred in the morning. The meeting had started at three o'clock and lasted until now, a little after six. It had not been a walk in the park. Don sat at the now-empty conference table, still reeling over the result: after three months' work, everything had ground to a halt. Faced with the prospect of moving on, the team had gone right back to the initial concerns he thought they'd all resolved.

"We're not going about this the right way," Sandra had said. "How do we really know a new series is the best answer? What about the brand equity we have in our existing title?"

"Right," someone else had chimed in. "We need more research on this."

Don wasn't quite sure what the outcome of the meeting had been, but he was fairly certain that it didn't fit Leonard's definition of "working things out."

•   •   •

How Grassroots Leaders Manage Work Horizontally

When it comes to managing work horizontally, successful leaders need to be resourceful and helpful. They need to know the system and how to get around it—in both senses of that term. If your ship went down and you ended up on a desert island, they are the kind of people you'd want to have with you—to get shelter organized, scrounge for sources of food, and set up a signaling system to attract would-be rescuers.

Cross-functional issues may be less life-threatening than being stranded on an island, but they're often no less daunting. When you try to manage work horizontally, you may find no supporting systems and procedures. Lines of authority may be tangled or nonexistent. The biggest hurdles, however, are generally created by all the departmental differences in priorities, values, technical knowledge, and ways of thinking.

To operate in this world, successful grassroots leaders seem to view the world through a versatile lens, one that can zoom in for close-ups, and then back way off for an all-encompassing panoramic shot. In other words, they have the outlook of systems thinkers, in that they have an ingrained interest in processes and how to improve them. On the other hand, because they also understand that they are themselves part of the process, they also know it's important to do their own work reliably, and to help others do theirs.

The best practices of grassroots leaders are as follows:

1. They take a bird's-eye view of work.

2. They are fierce managers of time.

3. They expedite cross-functional efforts.

4. They are willing to stay open-minded and suspend judgment.

Grassroots Leaders Take a Bird's-Eye View of Work

The behaviors around this best practice encompass both overarching systems thinking and hands-on practicality. Basically, successful leaders see problems as intriguing puzzles with many different pieces, some of which may seem to contradict each other at first. They always try to position themselves so that they will never be surprised, or blindsided, or tempted into plunging ahead before they have the full picture. In the words of Merry Goodenough, an assistant district counsel with the U.S. Army Corps of Engineers in San Francisco, "One of my goals is to communicate how the situation is going to impact [all our constituents]. Once I find a methodology to solve the problem, I don't just go off and solve it. I also disseminate the information, keeping in mind that everybody's individual story is only one piece of the puzzle."

Seek Out Multiple Perspectives

Taking this approach is especially helpful when you're solving problems of long standing. These have often persisted so long because they are rooted in several departments. This was the case in a critical incident set in a financial organization. The respondent described how an accountant got "fed up with an ongoing problem in the billing process. So he went around to other people who were being affected. He solved the problem by getting them in on it."

Another reason to seek out multiple perspectives is illustrated by a new production manager in a high-tech manufacturing organization who knew enough to know what he didn't know. "He admitted that he didn't know enough about how things worked to set up the new production process," wrote a respondent. "So he quickly identified key people to assist in this task, made sure everyone involved had a clear mission and offered his support to accomplish the task. The implementation of the new process has been very smooth and no one involved has had any complaints or misunderstandings."

A similar manufacturing incident about designing custom equipment underscores the importance of seeking out the right perspectives to make sure you have the complete picture. Faced with a very tight deadline, a ceramic engineer "did a great job of getting all the relevant stakeholders [involved]," wrote a respondent. "This was not off-the-shelf equipment, so good leadership was crucial to get through the design stages quickly and efficiently, making sure all input was considered. Coordinating the events from design to building to testing online was done wonderfully."

Go out of Your Way to Solve "White-Space" Problems

None of the successful leaders in our critical incidents took an it's-not-my-job,-it's-your-job approach to their work—not even in those handoff areas between one department and the next, in which there is usually plenty of legitimate confusion. In one incident, a marketing team realized that the way they organized their invoices totally befuddled the people in Finance who were responsible for paying them. Rather than joining with others to complain that Finance just didn't "get it," the marketing lead worked it out. Wrote the respondent, "He took a process that was confusing, walked through it, researched it, and redid it completely. Invoices now get paid correctly the first time and it makes everyone happy."

Perhaps because of their bird's-eye view, successful grassroots leaders will often see a need that others don't—for a new process to solve a problem, perhaps, or for a specific change that would produce more results. In one critical incident at a newly merged bank, employees from partner banks didn't seem enthusiastic about the merger, nor were they working together very productively. The training coordinator of the merger team pinpointed the problem as the lack of a process for integrating employees. "After collecting data and feedback," wrote the respondent, "she called a brainstorming meeting. . . . She brought all the right areas together and facilitated the development of an action plan. We now have a process in place that helps us more effectively integrate our newly merged employees into our organization."

If there is no useful process to help departments work together, the result can be acrimony, delays, and loss of revenue. One critical incident described how two individual contributors failed to work out a process to launch a new product, and as a result it was substantially delayed. "The deadline for getting the new product out slipped and then slipped again," the respondent wrote. "There was no established process for deciding when a product was OK and ready to be released.

The marketing person, who is a perfectionist, kept badgering the product designer to add more features. The product designer didn't speak up for himself. The situation went on for months. The product designer did not show leadership."

As the respondent noted, "It's easy to be a leader when there is a process, but when there isn't a process, then it's not quite so easy. You have to pull the right people together and say, 'OK, can we agree on a process here that's going to take us to the conclusion that we need?' The product designer didn't do that."

Grassroots Leaders Are Fierce Managers of Time

An intriguing theme running through our study is the increasingly high value people today place on time. They make a strong connection between leadership and time: they appreciate leaders who respect their time, and judge leaders harshly who waste it. The people in the critical incidents often seem literally thirsty for time. They seem to regard having their time wasted in much the same way a man in the desert would regard having his water spilled. It would be interesting to know if people considered time management such a key leadership skill 10 years ago.

According to the critical incidents, grassroots leaders get good marks in time management by:

- Helping others find legitimate shortcuts, especially with routine manual work

- Planning and executing their own work so they don't trip others up, or create emergencies other people have to bail them out of

- Not wasting other people's time with their own lack of preparedness

- Going out of their way to prevent duplicated effort

Find Ways to Save Others' Time

People remember leaders who make an effort to save them time, as in the following example concerning new financial software. "We had been very dissatisfied with the old system," the respondent wrote. "Our accountant did a lot of research to make sure the new system would allow us to bring over the old files, and switch back and forth without having to log in and out. We save time now, and have better productivity."

Even when people believe that these time-saving efforts are motivated primarily by cost or productivity concerns, they still seem to appreciate the positive impact on their own work. As one respondent put it, "Our new assistant director of marketing implemented a way to cut down and computerize paperwork that was time-consuming. It took a big workload off me."

Once again, leadership behavior is not limited to managers or supervisors. One respondent cited a hospital clerk who scheduled surgery. "She attempted to establish workload balance by monitoring doctors' loads regarding epidural blocks," the respondent observed. "She tracked records and was able to more effectively schedule the doctors' time. The new system she put in place makes the workload more even and balanced for the doctors."

Even small time-saving improvements were recalled as examples of leadership: "The secretary in our office created a form for us to use to help ensure accuracy of information. It saves time and money."

The negative examples describe the impact on others of a leader's lack of organization and failure to plan. A secretary was not fondly remembered for putting off an important mailing to the last minute: "Her actions created a rush. Eight of us had to drop everything we were doing and spend two hours stuffing envelopes."

In another incident, the manager of a real estate office talked people onto a project team without being honest about how much time would be involved. "Once they're involved, she gives them unrealistic timelines," said the respondent. "The result has been wasted time, poor morale and a lot of questions about the person's management abilities."

Although people recognize that everyone's job has become more complex, they don't accept this fact as an excuse to waste other people's time. A coworker described with some disdain the behavior of a government analyst who did exactly that: "It's true that he had been given a multitude of jobs. [However,] he got behind because he couldn't decide which job was most important. So things got put off to the last minute and then some jobs became urgent and the rest of us would have to take time off our jobs to keep his jobs on track."

When a formal leader seems to lack the ability to plan ahead—or, worse, doesn't take the trouble to do so—the people in these incidents feel that no one is watching out for them, and they resent it. Their work is hard enough, they seem to be saying, without having to contend with a "dingbat" at the helm. This disgusted attitude is evident in the person who wrote, "The supervisor of our college's reprographics department knew at least six weeks ahead of time that the temporary worker was leaving, [but] . . . by the time he got someone else hired there was no one around to provide training. There was a complete lapse of coverage in the department. Computer files could not be found. Items were not ready when they were due. The new person didn't know anything about policies, procedures, equipment, or billing."

Don't Set People Up to Work at Cross-Purposes

People become angry when they discover they've been given work that duplicates the efforts of others. In many cases their anger comes less from having their time wasted than from feeling discounted by a leader's failure to make sure their efforts were not in vain. "For some reason, our senior manager assigned projects to several areas with conflicting priorities and information," wrote someone who works in a financial institution. "This move wasted our time and our efforts. We feel very frustrated and resentful."

Another incident from a high-tech company echoes this frustration: "We realized that we had three groups in three areas working on the same goal. Our work should be coordinated— but the team lead did nothing about the situation. We still have three groups doing three different things, so we are really accomplishing nothing."

Be Prepared

If you're going to inform or train other people, they expect you to be prepared. Two of the critical incidents provide a study in contrasts in this regard. In one, an administrative assistant in a government agency was unable to explain a provision of a welfare reform proposal to other staff members, even though she was responsible for doing so. "It was clear she didn't know what she was talking about," the respondent wrote. "The other staffers knew more than she did. They interrupted and attacked her." It's worth noting that when she tried to participate later in the meeting, the others ignored her. Her failure to prepare herself had apparently cost her whatever authority she started the meeting with.

In contrast, an incident about a purchasing agent in another government agency illustrates how much people appreciate leaders who take the time to do their homework. "We needed to make some decisions about some property, [and] we had asked him to get us some facts and figures," wrote a respondent. "He came to our meeting with maps and charts and was able to answer all our questions. Because he was so well prepared, we were able to make quick decisions, and put a plan together on how we were going to purchase the land and what funds we will be using."

Grassroots Leaders Expedite Cross-Functional Efforts

It may be a testimony to the challenge of managing work horizontally that many of these critical incidents refer to a point in a project when even the most independent people want a leader to just take over. At these moments they don't want to be listened to, or coached, or painted into anyone's picture of the future—they want someone else to get behind the wheel and drive the project for a while. Sometimes what they want most is for a leader to demonstrate his or her commitment, and to get a firsthand appreciation for the challenges they're facing. At other times they may need concrete help in overcoming a hurdle or keeping the momentum going. The challenge is to know when it's time to get help, and then to have the courage to keep pushing for help until you get it.

Take Serious Deadlines Seriously

There may be nothing more important to an organization's fiscal well-being than having a product hit the market on schedule. In one critical incident, a rollout involving several departments had a tight deadline. The team needed a single source of current and accurate data that all appropriate team members could access. "A marketing support person jumped into this mess," a respondent reported. "She took it upon herself to go to all departments outside her own and figure out what information needed to be shared. She quickly put a process in place to make sure the right data went to the right people. Thanks largely to her efforts, the product was rolled out on schedule."

Grassroots leaders are also good at protecting project deadlines from "project creep." Sometimes a leader must take a stand—and stick to it. The following incident illustrates what a successful leader did to lay the groundwork that enabled his ultimatum to pay off. At issue was a product rollout thousands of dollars and months over budget. A new manager was brought in with a new deadline to enforce. "First I talked to each department head, and made sure I understood their concerns," he said. "I learned that Marketing kept wanting new features, which Engineering would only add if it could test them adequately. The more testing Engineering did, the more time they gave Marketing to think of new features. So I brought them all together, and said we were freezing the product specs, and launching the product next Wednesday. I actually think they were relieved."

Demonstrate Commitment

People need tangible evidence of a leader's commitment to a course of action; words alone are seldom enough. For example, small colleges often talk about the need to generate more community support; in one incident, a dean at a southern college did something about it. "He came up with the idea of a promotional insert in the local paper," said the respondent. "He arranged a meeting with newspaper reps and was able to identify over two hundred companies that could be solicited to buy advertising space in the insert. This was a great promotional effort. It did not require college funds, it provided broad distribution of information about the college, and it boosted morale on campus."

Unfortunately, more of the critical incidents in our research make this point through negative examples. In one incident at an engineering firm, a supervisor assigned an engineer to document the technical requirements for a new product. The supervisor said the project was important, but failed to back up his words with action. "Even though the deadline was very short," the respondent said, "the supervisor did not provide the background information or contacts the engineer needed to get started. [At the very last minute] the supervisor provided additional resources to make the scheduled deadline, but in the meantime, working relationships throughout the whole section had become very tense."

In a critical incident from an insurance company, a leader's failure to support his project caused its eventual demise. "An underwriter had been assigned to run a major study," wrote a respondent. "He handed out assignments to each member, but he provided no guidance or follow-up. He delegated everything, but didn't retain control or authority." Not surprisingly, the study fell apart and was never completed.

Relish the Details of Project Management

The following critical incidents illustrate how much people appreciate leaders who aren't too proud to track a project's details, which might otherwise drift off the radar screen. In the words of a respondent describing a marketing manager at a utility, "She not only took charge of the project and made wise decisions. She followed up on all the details."

It's evident that, although some managers may see themselves as "big-concept people," respondents appreciate a leader who is detail-oriented. In an incident that makes this point, a training manager in an insurance company skillfully organized a very large project. Said the respondent, "We are preparing for a major system conversion. Our group will be training over 500 employees at five different sites. With input from our team, my manager has done an incredible job of identifying what needs to be done, assigning responsibility and then following up to check on the status of many details. We have assumed responsibility for what needs to get done because we know it's important to her and she will be checking back."

An accounting manager in a real estate firm got down into the pine needles to solve a problem that had been going on for over a year. "Even though it was not a part of his normal duties, he got all the facts, made a timeline, delegated, and followed it up," noted the respondent. "The problem was divided out so that Accounts Payable, General Ledger, and Closing each took care of their part. It produced a positive outflow in the whole area."

People involved in a new venture are usually reassured by having a structured approach they can follow, as long as it's not too rigid. A team leader in a manufacturing organization reduced the anxiety about implementing a new program by volunteering to create a responsibility matrix, which would clarify roles for all department team leaders. "The team leader's manager felt relieved because he hadn't had time to do appropriate planning," wrote the respondent.

Know How to Get a Project Back on Track

As these incidents reveal, there are many different ways a project can run out of steam, and successful grassroots leaders are able to deal with all of them. One incident at a health care organization praised a vice president for breathing life back into a stalled effort. "He was a good facilitator for the project. This project was at the point where it had kind of stagnated and someone needed to get it going again and see it to its end. The project was seen through and is functioning today."

Although not a formal leader, a staff accountant in a distribution company showed similar initiative "by taking it upon herself to get the project out of a dead end. She didn't depend on her supervisor to bail her out." In another situation, a data-entry coordinator played a significant role in getting her project back on track, primarily by tracking and following up on details that reinforced the team's focus. "There were a lot of changes taking place in our project. It was hard to keep track of them all. She acted as facilitator for the team. She made a list of things to be done, prioritized them into a calendar and wrote up the minutes of each meeting with a synopsis of what had to be done for each person, and gave one to each team member. She constantly kept us on target."

On the other hand, although people praise grassroots leaders for resuscitating projects, they also criticize leaders for keeping a project on life support that deserves to die. "The director of marketing neglected to cancel or redesign a project that was obviously failing," said one respondent. "I believe that canceling the project, which was very popular, would have made the person look like a leader, but she was probably afraid she'd look like a bad guy."

It's also possible to do too much bird-dogging. "She means well, but she pesters people," wrote a respondent from an insurance agency about one of her colleagues. "We don't even bother to keep track of things, because we know she'll always tell us what to do."

Know When to Bump Problems Up

Delegating upward is traditionally seen as a sign of failure, but in today's world it's often the most expedient way to move forward. This is especially true during a merger or other major change, when life is chaotic and there can be a great deal of slippage between the conditions that apply when an assignment is given and when it's carried out. In one incident, a team leader from a manufacturing facility trying to reduce cycle time realized that her team could not meet a drop-dead deadline unless they shaved product quality. Heart in her throat, she went to her manager, and expressed her concerns. She was convinced she was making a career-limiting move, and that he would think she was either criticizing his plan, or else was a poor project manager. However, all he said was, "OK sure, go ahead and change it."

In another incident, reality dashed cold water on a project leader at the end of his first team meeting, when he asked everyone to get their calendars out to schedule the next meeting. It turned out one person was about to take a sabbatical, another was going on vacation, and a third was really busy with another project. In fact, there was only one day in the next six weeks when they could all get together. "The project leader went to the person he was accountable to and explained the situation, and suggested they renegotiate a later project deadline when members would be more available. Somehow this manager magically got team members more released time, or else found others to replace them."

•   •   •

During the weekend after Don's disastrous meeting, some bad weather blew into town, and Don found himself hoping that it might develop into a hurricane that would obliterate all evidence of this project. By Monday morning, however, the winds and rain had diminished, and he was once again faced with what he had come to believe was either a career-destroying assignment or the world's greatest opportunity for personal growth. After his first cup of coffee he stopped by Leonard's office. He had a trial balloon he wanted to float by his boss.

"Maybe Sandra's right," Don said. "Maybe it doesn't make sense to develop a new series. Maybe we should stick with what works. Just update it."

"You're changing your mind?" Leonard leaned forward in his chair. "You know, the people in the field really are looking for something new."

"Updating would definitely be an easier row to hoe," Don said. "I ask myself why are they being so resistant to change, but then I say, hey, maybe this isn't a change issue at all. The product sold all those copies. How wrong-headed can they be for wanting to preserve it? Maybe it's me."

"Hm."

"Then I start thinking Sandra and her cohorts are hatching plots to sabotage me. Like maybe they secretly went to these managers and got them to yank their people off the team."

Leonard frowned. "You don't really believe that. Do you?"

"I don't know!" Don was pacing. "It's getting so I don't trust my own judgment, you know what I mean? I mean, where's the reality here?"

Leonard tapped his pencil on the desk. "I think that's a question we're all trying to answer."

•   •   •

Grassroots Leaders Are Willing to Stay Open and Suspend Their Judgment

A reading of the critical incidents for this strategy suggests that successful grassroots leaders have found ways to set aside their

traditional departmental and work group loyalties, at least as far
as their cross-functional work is concerned. Adopting a more
inclusive view enables leaders to avoid divisive actions based on
biased judgments. At the same time, however, suspended judgment can feel like no judgment, and when there are several conflicting views to contend with, it's easy to lose your grounding. "I
keep telling myself Purchasing does things differently," said a manufacturing engineer who's serving on a cross-functional team to
improve purchasing procedures. "I have to believe they have a
good reason for doing what I can't help thinking seems stupid."

The most successful leaders are able to maintain an attitude
that other departments are not wrong; they just do things differently. In one example, this difference seemed to be about
time. Wrote one respondent who was a member of a cross-
functional team, "The people from the other department were
always late with their assignments. I guess they must have
thought they had all the time in the world. Instead of nagging
them to do their work on time, the project leader would go to
them way before an assignment was due and ask if they saw
any obstacles, or if their workload might change."

•   •   •

Don was sick of leaders with more questions than answers.
Back in his office, he spread out the timeline he had prepared
for this project, and spent an hour taking a close look at every
item on it. This exercise produced some brain-clearing conclusions. Even though he had not been able to work things out
with Sandra "at their level," at this point it didn't really matter
why. Nor did it matter where the "reality" was, or whether this
was a change issue or a brand equity issue, or whether more
research was needed. What mattered at this point was that if
something didn't change drastically right now, the team would
not meet the publication date for this series. The date had
been announced to great fanfare, and revenue projections had
been built into the budget.

Talk about focusing on the bottom line, Don thought as he
dialed Leonard's extension. Leonard answered on the first ring,
almost as if he had been waiting for the call, and listened atten-
tively while Don made his case.

"What would you like me to do?" he asked when Don had finished.

"I think you need to work this out at *your* level," Don said, "so we can work it out at *ours*."

There was a long pause. "OK," Don thought, "this is it. I'm asking Mr. Delegator to bail me out. This is where I get dragged off the project in disgrace."

Leonard finally spoke. "So it feels like you've been set up for failure?"

"Uh . . . well, yeah."

"OK," Leonard said. "Well, look. Why don't you and I get together and do some strategizing so we can get this project moving?"

"Now?"

"Why not? And don't worry. We'll figure out a way to make this happen. I promise."

•   •   •

Grassroots Leadership Step by Step

The following is a list of tools that can help you better manage work horizontally. These are located in the section called "Tools: Grassroots Leadership Step by Step" (pages 168–187).

Managing Your Priorities (Tool 12).   This tool will help you handle conflicting demands so you can concentrate your best efforts where they are most needed. Included are steps to clarify expectations for a task you've been assigned, cope with overload, and hand off a task to someone else (pages 168–172).

Influencing for Win-Win Outcomes (Tool 13).   The steps in this tool help you present your ideas to other people in ways that respond to their needs, so that they will be motivated to give you their support (pages 173–178).

"Team Formation Checklist" (Tool 14).   Use this list of key questions to help identify the challenges for a team in several situations: when it starts a new project, changes goals or plans, doesn't meet deadlines, has a new leader, or needs to clarify roles and responsibilities (pages 179–181).

Raising Difficult Issues with Your Team (Tool 15). This tool provides specific actions you can take to communicate honestly, define the scope of a problem, and gain the commitment you need from team members to reach a solution (pages 182–187).

 To get results in today's looser, less hierarchical organizations, grassroots leaders take a project-oriented, cross-functional approach to work. Successful grassroots leaders are helpful and resourceful. Whereas they have the systems thinker's ability to see how the parts fit into the whole, they also always carry their own weight. Their work is reliable; they don't need others to rescue them from emergencies. They concentrate their efforts on the following best practices:

1. They take a bird's-eye view of work.
2. They are fierce managers of time.
3. They expedite cross-functional efforts.
4. They are willing to stay open-minded and suspend judgment.

CHAPTER

6

Build Credibility
and Trust

*Twenty-three percent of all incidents, the second largest
group after "involve every mind," fell into this category.
They included six competencies: "Take initiative beyond
job requirements;" "Take responsibility for your own
actions and the actions of your group;" "Handle
emotions in yourself and others;" "Display professional
ethics;" "Show compassion;" and "Make credible
presentations." The incidents were evenly divided
between management and nonmanagement examples.*

THIS IS THE CLIMB STRATEGY YOU DON'T EXECUTE OR CARRY OUT—
you demonstrate. You do so by taking a series of unannounced
personal tests, most of which take place in public, and some of
which you may have to go looking for. You either pass or fail;
there is no middle ground. Pass, and your credibility and trust
are enhanced, or at least maintained. Fail—even once—and
they are damaged, in some cases permanently. Furthermore, if

you don't show up, you automatically fail, and there's no time available to schedule makeups.

This is the harsh and unforgiving picture to emerge from an analysis of the critical incidents for this strategy, which represent almost one-quarter of the total number collected for the study itself.

The tests in the critical incidents focus on a leader's ability to make the right choice in difficult situations—rather than opting for the easy or safe choice, or avoiding a choice altogether. In most cases, there's a certain amount of risk involved; otherwise, it wouldn't be a test. Although the tests aren't physical, the critical incidents often describe them in physical terms (for example, "step in" or "go out on a limb"), and leaders often pass by working extra hard.

What drives this testing process is the human need to trust and respect the leaders into whose hands we deliver ourselves. The less familiar and more treacherous the journey, the more we want to make sure our leaders are up to the task. We want a leader with the necessary technical expertise, but what we want most is someone with *the right stuff.* This is what the people in the critical incidents are looking for in their leaders. They are energized and reassured when they see it, and disillusioned and even frightened when they don't.

These critical incidents seem to describe a leader's behavior in more nuanced detail than those for the other strategies. This suggests the incidents themselves carry an emotional weight that makes them memorable. Perhaps as a result, people pay closer attention to the leader's behavior; the more difficult the situation, the more microscopic their evaluation. Respondents often say they learned something new about a leader during these moments, both hitherto unnoticed cracks in their facade as well as hidden strengths.

In a sense, this strategy expresses in behavioral terms the abstract concept of leadership "character." We can't know from the critical incidents whether the people they describe have such a character. What we do know is that the men and women who do a good job with the six related competencies are seen by respondents as leaders worth following. Those leaders who mess up or neglect the competencies—especially at critical moments—not only earn other people's disapproval and scorn, but also their reluctance or outright refusal to cast their lot with such untrustworthy characters.

If you are one of those people who tend to look inside yourself and worry if you have the character to be an effective leader—if you wonder whether you're made of the right stuff—these incidents contain both bad news and good news. The bad news is that this is the strategy most difficult to fake. It's the one that is most likely to reveal who you really are, the one in which your behavior at work is probably most similar to your behavior at home and elsewhere in your life. The good news is that at least you're not being judged against some ill-defined abstract moral or psychological standard, but on how well you perform six specific competencies. In other words, rather than looking inward for the right stuff, look instead for opportunities to take initiative, take responsibility for your actions, handle emotions, display professional ethics, show compassion, and make credible presentations. Do these well, and others will see you as a credible and trustworthy leader.

When Leaders Aren't Credible or Trustworthy

In today's flatter and looser organizations, positional authority (the title on your door) is on its way to becoming less important than personal clout, the biggest part of which is your credibility and trustworthiness. For both managers and nonmanagers, these may ultimately turn out to be your only significant sources of power, the only way you have to marshal resources and convince people to follow your lead—especially if you're working cross-functionally. Without personal credibility, you may feel as if you have to make twice the effort to cover half the ground.

What's more, you may never know why. In the first place, we tend to think of ourselves as credible and trustworthy people, even though other people might not always experience us that way. Furthermore, personal credibility seems to be a dimension of leadership people are reluctant to give feedback about, perhaps because they assume negative behavior is evidence of a basic character flaw, which their feedback could do little to correct.

The raft of bad behavior with which leaders discredit themselves in these incidents includes lying, emotional eruptions, ducking responsibility, blaming others, stealing others' ideas, and passing the buck. Transgressions like these create a toxic fog of blaming and defensiveness that kills off the willingness to try anything new, or put in extra effort. People feel confused and scared, almost as if they've been abandoned—especially during times of change and upheaval, when the only thing that may keep them on an even keel are words of assurance from a leader they believe in and trust.

How Grassroots Leaders Build Credibility and Trust

The successful grassroots leaders in these critical incidents never seem to be off duty; when presented with opportunities to test themselves they seem prepared or at least willing to take a chance. They demonstrate an ability to walk the line between playing it too safe and going too far. Although there's no way to tell if they consciously seek out occasions to demonstrate their credibility, they do seem to make the most of the occasions that come their way.

There is a definite heroic flavor to the positive critical incidents. Successful grassroots leaders—at least those who get noticed by others—do the right thing at the right time, even though there is often some risk involved. They are willing to take on challenges they think are important, and to do so in public without any guarantee they will be successful. Although their efforts might fall short of what Superman might do, they nevertheless earn the trust of those around them. The best practices they follow—the areas in which they concentrate their efforts—are as follows:

1. They make credible presentations.
2. They do the right thing.
3. They take on tough challenges.
4. They leverage strong emotions.
5. They believe in themselves.

Grassroots Leaders Make Credible Presentations

What the emergence of this competency seems to indicate is that, whether it's actually true, people think good speakers make good leaders. Public speaking is certainly seen to be risky behavior; there's research to show that many people fear speaking in public more than death. Speaking in public also presents the opportunity to demonstrate credibility, especially when the leader speaks from the heart.

Several incidents praise leaders who appear to be telling the whole story without holding anything back. In one, a CEO demonstrated his credibility by dealing with tough issues honestly and without fear. "In front of 200 employees our CEO addressed hard questions and admitted that he didn't have all the answers," wrote one respondent. "This was done with credible emotion and enthusiasm that energized the audience and caused them to rally together in support of the business objectives. I think the key behaviors on his part were openness, fearlessness (he was willing to address whatever came up), credible emotion, and concern for people in addition to the business."

People seem almost in awe of leaders who can present bad news or criticism in a way that people will hear. Colm Gorman, in the training department at Intel Ireland Ltd., cites the manager of manufacturing for his ability to be direct with operators during his regularly scheduled meetings with them. "He'll talk about what they're doing well, but sometimes he also has very strong messages to get across," says Gorman, "like housekeeping or safety issues. I've seen other people try this, and it comes across as a mixed message. He has a very powerful but effective way of doing it. You'd think they'd walk out of the room cursing him, but they don't."

People suspect that when leaders hold back or don't communicate clearly, they may have something to hide or haven't done their homework. As one person wrote, "The director did not communicate important facts about a department's change in organizational structure. He had a rapid-fire style of communicating the change [which left] little opportunity to ask questions. There was also no explanation of why these changes were taking place or how they were decided upon."

In one case a leader's body language caused him to flunk the credibility test. "When he finally met with us, he failed to make any eye contact as he delivered his message," wrote the respondent. "This was perceived as the leader holding back information. He left us feeling that we could not trust him in the future."

Good speaking skills can reinforce your message—and your status as a leader. A city government employee said as much in describing the city manager. "Forceful, but easy to relate to, not demeaning in tone or content, enthusiastic, believable at all levels—this was our 'CEO' speaking," said the employee. "It made me feel good about the organization. I agree with his message." In another incident, a leader made a short 15-minute speech in which he "reviewed the company's accomplishments for last year, and its goals and objectives for the coming year. Everyone knows where to focus. It shows good leadership."

By the same token, people also seem to assume that if a leader can't make a good presentation, he or she might not be capable of doing much else, either. As one respondent reported, "He gave a presentation in an area of his expertise, but he seemed not only unprepared, but also uncertain of himself. Some members of the audience questioned his competency and expertise. We are hesitant to utilize him with our clients."

Grassroots Leaders Do the Right Thing

There was a theme in these incidents of making the right choice, doing what is right instead of what is easy or expedient.

Handle Tough Performance Issues

Over and over, incidents made the point that handling performance issues can be unpleasant and tempting to ignore. Nevertheless, this is a responsibility people expect leaders to fulfill, as the following example illustrates. "Someone was not carrying their load and the supervisor had to step in," wrote the respondent. "The situation was getting worse and people were complaining because they had to do more work, so their supervisor had to do something. The worker is getting better and everyone is happier."

Leaders will probably be chagrined to know how easily people see through their excuses for not stepping in to address a performance problem. "Two of our business 'leaders' knew a particular contractor had been very indecisive throughout the order processing," the respondent began. "Instead of demonstrating positive leadership skills, both of these upper-level managers passed the responsibility back and forth until they 'decided' the best thing would be to 'let go' of the situation and let some lower-level people bear the burden.

"These lower-level people are handling the situation the best they can, but feel as though they have no support from the top, and that upper management has no backbone. They feel there is no direction in the organization and they have to put out fires on their own."

Take the Blame, Even if It Isn't Your Fault

If people only knew how much respect they get for standing up and taking the blame, especially when it's not their fault, more of them would undoubtedly do so. In fact, the people in our study regard taking the blame—or refusing to take the blame—as a defining leadership moment.

Some of the incidents were positive. A supervisor at a health services organization earned high marks. "He took responsibility for a mistake made by someone else in the department under his area of supervision. It was an ad that didn't get placed and the supervisor took the blame for it. The supervisor later met with the employee to get better communication so it wouldn't happen again."

A marketing manager gained respect when he accepted responsibility for an error. "It was a group error," noted the respondent. "He took it upon himself as a representative of the company—even though he didn't actually make the error himself. He realized that whenever something goes wrong, even though it may not appear to be his fault, it is his fault."

In describing a vice president at a financial institution, a respondent linked his behaviors to very positive outcomes: "If something went wrong, he would not point fingers, but accepted responsibility and handled problems in a diplomatic and effective way. He was an excellent leader because of this.

Everyone on his staff respected him, looked up to him, and tried their hardest to follow his lead and do a good job for him."

Unfortunately, many more of the critical incidents describe leaders who not only avoid blame themselves, but point fingers at others. The respondents obviously find this behavior distasteful. "The director used the supervisor as a public scapegoat to avoid taking responsibility for failure in his area. He told everyone else he was demoting this supervisor before he told the supervisor himself. We lost respect and trust for the director."

It may be human nature to resist accepting responsibility for one's mistakes, from a fear of punishment, perhaps, or a reluctance to look incompetent. The critical incidents, however, paint a very negative picture of such behavior. "A department supervisor did not meet his production goals and he publicly blamed his employees and peers. So what he got was mistrust from his peers and reduced cooperation from his employees."

Judging from these incidents, people in upper management seem just as tempted to weasel out of responsibility as anyone else. "Our manufacturing director attended a continuous improvement team meeting as a representative of upper management," wrote a respondent from a manufacturing company. "Instead of responding to the concerns of the team, he placed blame on a member of his own department. In effect, he abdicated any responsibility for the issue discussed. Team members, particularly the hourly employees on the team, lost respect for this individual and the way he managed his department. The team refused to accept his answers as representative of management, and appealed to a higher authority."

In addition to destroying his or her personal credibility, a leader who doesn't own up can set a tone that may damage the reputation of an entire team or work group. This was the assessment of an IT professional, who wrote, "While changing to a new computer database, there were some unexpected problems. Instead of taking a leadership role, everyone pointed fingers at someone else, including our manager. Our department's credibility is very low. It's embarrassing to be part of this group."

When a team leader points fingers at a team member, he or she can destroy in one moment the team spirit that may have

taken months to develop. An incident of this type occurred at
a utility company, triggered by the CEO's sharp questioning of
the leader of an acquisitions team. The CEO wanted to know
why the acquisition team had paid so much for a new acquisition. "The team leader 'pointed the finger' at one part of the
team—distancing himself from the problem," the respondent
wrote. "The team effort fell apart."

Finally, if you're going to take the blame, it seems important to
take it fully, without mincing words or using legalistic language.
The public relations director of a hospital issued a half-apology
that made matters worse than they were before. "She prepared a
press release concerning an upcoming event," the respondent
wrote, "but did not confirm the content of the release with the
appropriate department manager. Unfortunately, the release contained an incorrect date. She then drafted a corrected release
and an apology. Although the apology was nicely worded, she
failed to accept full responsibility for her lapse, instead placing
the blame on 'misinformation provided from the department
manager.' Bad feelings now exist between the department manager and the public relations director. A lack of trust is evident."

Don't Desert the Ship

The following incident about an operations manager in an east-
ern manufacturing company would be almost funny if its
impact were not so serious. "Our operation was in a start-up
mode," said a supervisor, one of the manager's direct reports.
"This is a very busy and sometimes troublesome period. Extra
help is always appreciated under stressful conditions. In this
case, [the operations manager] wished us all good luck and
took advantage of a sunny afternoon to go fishing! As the frontline supervisor, I was stunned. When this operation is down,
we lose money! My operators wondered why he was still
employed the following day. He lost the respect of my crew
and myself."

Don't Drop the Ball

There was a slew of negative incidents that indicted not only
managers but also individual contributors for poor leadership

behavior—not finishing work, unloading work onto others, and refusing to help. Here are some representative voices:

- "The energy consultant dropped the ball on a project and didn't take full responsibility for it. The supervisor had to finish the project to ensure that it was complete."

- "We have a slide presentation of our company's history, and our business graphics technicians wouldn't take the responsibility to update it. There was no one else to do it."

- "I went to one of our accounting clerks for help because I couldn't reconcile the payroll. He didn't know the answer, so he pushed it onto someone else instead of trying to get the answer for me."

In a more serious incident, a respondent laid the blame for people losing jobs at the feet of an HR specialist who dropped the ball. "Because our company lost a major contract, there were going to be a lot of layoffs. However, a lot of other divisions within the company were hiring. The HR specialist didn't take the initiative to contact the divisions that were hiring. She dumped it; she didn't follow through. Because of her inaction, a lot of people didn't have an opportunity to apply for positions in other company divisions. People lost jobs."

Demonstrate Professional Ethics

The considerable number of incidents that make this point are all negative. They depict leaders lying, taking credit for someone else's work, making false accusations, showing favoritism, revealing private information, and even harassing others. This is serious stuff. It seems unlikely any of the leaders in these incidents will ever be able to recover the personal credibility and trust their behavior cost them. "What were they thinking?" is the question that comes to mind. They not only didn't demonstrate professional ethics, they didn't demonstrate much common sense, either.

Lying tops the list of trust destroyers. A college dean who lied to get out of a tight spot went from the frying pan into the fire. This example shows how people can interpret a single transgression as evidence of a much larger character flaw. "The dean is not truthful to those who report to him," the respondent claims. "He needed to explain the reason for a decision and basically told a lie to deflect pressures off of himself. His employees don't trust him anymore."

In another situation, an HR manager's lie tainted her whole department in the eyes of the respondent. "She said something to me both of us knew was untrue, and she showed favoritism to a company (vendor) that I feel has dealt fraudulently with us. I don't trust her and don't believe in her integrity. I now even doubt the whole HR system in our company."

Another fast way to destroy your credibility is to betray confidences and use poor judgment concerning sensitive information. One incident cited an HR person (of all people!) for breaking a confidence. "She gossiped, and gave out information that should have been kept confidential. We now lack respect and trust for her," the respondent said. In another example, a respondent thought a manager had been irresponsible in divulging corporate information prematurely. "He shared information with the staff that should not have been shared, and made promises about rewards that employees would be getting in the future for their work. Employee expectations were heightened too much."

One leader's cavalier treatment of information was apparently so flagrant he drove an employee out of the company. "A manager wrote a memo accusing another manager of creating problems with employees," the respondent reported. "This memo was copied and widely distributed throughout the organization. It was then discovered that all of the allegations were untrue. The person who was falsely accused was so upset by the incident that he resigned. We lost a very good employee."

A big part of being ethical is being fair and consistent. In the following incident the supervisor's inconsistency, which is apparently nothing more than forgetfulness, has a very negative impact on her work group. "Awhile ago she told the employees in a staff meeting that no one could have a Monday or Friday off unless it was an emergency," the respondent wrote. "But by now she's forgotten this rule. She lets some people take Monday or Friday off just by asking. Other people first have to find another employee to work that day. This place has low morale, inconsistency, confusion, and uncertainty."

And yes, there were incidents about sexual harassment. "This person made threats indirectly to a member of the opposite sex, trying to intimidate them and impress them," said one respondent. "Being in a leadership role, that's not something that represents a company very well or gives a company a good name."

Show Compassion

People see compassion and caring as an important part of leadership, whether it occurs at work or elsewhere. Some of the following incidents are gestures; others are larger efforts. They all created a positive and lasting impact.

- "She was moving and couldn't afford another vacation day, so the supervisor let her have one of his."

- An administrative assistant took it upon herself to organize a fund-raiser for a children's organization. "Our company knew the charity needed help. She just took on the whole job."

- On the caring behavior of a guard at a hospital: "For example, he will hold an umbrella for someone if it's raining so they can get into their car without getting wet," the respondent observed. "When a visitor was holding a baby and his shoe lace was untied, the guard bent down to tie it. He is naturally a caring person."

Grassroots Leaders Take On Tough Challenges

In addition to doing the right thing when situations present themselves, grassroots leaders also seem to go looking for opportunities to help. When there's a potential risk involved, people tend to see these efforts as especially strong evidence of personal credibility. Behavior is often expressed in physical terms: leaders "jump in." They "dig in." They "step up." They "go out on a limb," and "do whatever it takes" to "save the day." Here are a few examples:

- "A young lady in manufacturing stepped into a supervisor role and kept the manufacturing process moving on the weekend shift."

- "An unscheduled mailing had to go out by [a certain time] and this person jumped right in and made it happen by the deadline."

- "Some members of a high-tech team took advantage of the fact that the supervisor wasn't in. They sat back and relaxed. The other team members pushed back on them and said they all should work. 'This is a chance to prove ourselves,' they said."

- "We were behind in getting files organized this year, and she took the initiative to help us do it. She's an assistant vice president; it was not her normal work. I thought it showed good leadership to dig in and help us."

Getting an unscheduled mailing out might not be heroic in the action-hero sense of the word, but such tasks are important to the respondents in our study, who are grateful when a leader volunteers to help out. However, if you're going to jump in, you'd better make sure you're helping and not meddling, as the following incident illustrates. "She took it upon herself to start going through the mail because she did not feel that one of the individuals was doing her part," the respondent wrote. "She did not take into consideration that she was stepping on other people's areas of authority. Even though she had good intentions, [she] basically started a civil war within the department. There was a lot of talking back and forth, and other departments took sides."

Take On Extra Work

For today's overworked employees, nothing seems more heroic or indicative of personal credibility than a leader's willingness to add to his or her workload. "We had a vacancy in the department," a respondent wrote from a Canadian hospital. "The field assistant took over that vacancy, plus his own position until that vacancy was filled." In another incident, when a colleague became ill, a nurse "stepped in to assume responsibility of two units so that no patients would go unattended and without care."

When someone acts with the welfare of other employees in mind, people see that as leadership, even if that person is not a formal leader. In one incident, a clerical employee decided to take over the responsibilities of her manager when she went on maternity leave, "so that the department would not fall behind and all the employees would receive their pay," wrote the respondent. "The department is running fine, and everyone is getting paid because she took over."

Taking on extra work to achieve an important goal lets everyone know how important you think it is. Wrote one respondent in this regard, "The quality assurance supervisor worked two shifts because the problems we were having affected the entire facility and she would not leave until the problem was resolved. Others were grateful for her efforts and she earned more respect."

Don't Be Fazed by Last-Minute Challenges

Organizational life today seems to consist of an endless series of changes in plans. People respect leaders who can roll with the punches, do what needs to be done, and not make a big fuss about it. "One of our engineers got a project for one of our biggest customers dropped in his lap at the last moment, and was given three days to get it done," noted a respondent. "He completed all engineering tasks as well as purchasing and manufacturing tasks. These tasks were not part of his assignment, but he knew the job had to be done and he rose to the occasion. The field installation went off very well. The efforts will maintain our commitment to our customers."

In this case, the leader would probably not have flunked the test if he had not accepted the new deadline, or had been unable to meet it, because it was generally agreed to be unreasonable. However, the fact that he successfully took on the challenge, even though he had a good excuse for avoiding it, gained him increased credibility.

In another incident, a respondent describes a frontline leader who successfully met challenges created by her own boss. "She showed outstanding leadership by effectively overcoming many obstacles thrown at her by her supervisor," the respondent wrote. "He was supposed to conduct training in Contracts, but with just two weeks' notice he asked her to do it instead. She put together a super package of two hundred pages plus an outline and overheads. She also ran an excellent class session."

Grassroots Leaders Leverage Strong Emotions

Successful grassroots leaders not only are able to control their own emotions, they are also comfortable working with the strong emotions of other people. The most successful leaders can channel the energy in emotional outbursts in more productive directions.

For many people, an out-of-control emotional situation is the organizational equivalent of the caveful of snakes in *Raiders of the Lost Ark*. They're frightened by emotional behavior that seems either out of control or on the edge. People expect leaders to be able to control their own tempers and to protect them from the emotionally violent outbursts of others. People are impressed by leaders who can stand up to strong emotions. They feel safer, and the leader looks stronger.

Don't Fly Off the Handle

When leaders don't control themselves, they're seen as unreliable and even dangerous. The following negative examples come from all industry sectors and from people at all levels of the organization:

- "He lost his temper and walked out of the management team meeting before the conclusion of the discussion. How can supposedly mature men revert to juvenile behavior?"

- "He lost his temper because some of his staff had a different opinion than his on a subject. He ended a staff conference call on a bad note and managed to lose considerable respect from his staff."

- "She lost her cool with a group of complaining employees and used swear words. People were upset and offended, especially at the use of God's name in that way. She lost respect."

- "In working on a project in the manager's absence, a staff member made a decision with which the manager did not agree. The manager became very emotional; he shouted and was accusatory. He finally calmed down and discussed the issue, but the damage was already done. The staff are reluctant to have one-on-one encounters with him. The atmosphere becomes very tense. The mood is apprehensive and accusatory."

The following incident should prove instructional for the frustrated leader who is sometimes tempted to stop pussyfooting around and read a few people the riot act. "The boss got very emotional," said the respondent about a leader who was not happy with his staff. "The shouting, banging on his desk, and threatening of his direct reports drove fear into the organization. He got total shutdown of input from his people. We now give the boss what the boss wants—even if it's the wrong thing to do. And six out of ten highly skilled supervisors have sought employment elsewhere!"

Know How to Calm Things Down

People seem to expect a leader to defuse an emotional situation. "The leader remained calm, cool, and collected during a 'heated,' highly emotional discussion," reported a respondent. "The rest of the group followed his lead and also calmed down."

People are reassured by a leader's ability to remain calm. In trying to read how upset a leader is (and therefore how upset they should be), people will tune into tone of voice, body language, gestures, and choice of words. In one incident, a CEO at an insurance company had to mediate an angry confrontation in a meeting of the executive team. "The head of the policy branch angrily accused his peer of not providing his operation the services it needed," the respondent wrote. "The CEO . . . stated in a professional tone the need for the two branches to work together to identify the problems, and seek solutions. The head of the policy branch's attitude changed from accusing to one of agreeing we all had to work together."

In another situation, a vice president used several techniques to calm down a meeting of 140 managers who went ballistic while discussing a new organization structure. "The vice president got up and talked to the group in a manner that created some intimacy between her and the managers," wrote the person reporting the incident. "She was able to bring the meeting back to some semblance of order and productiveness. She answered each concern with direct eye contact, talked about potential advantages and disadvantages, shared her experience at other companies where this had worked, solicited input, and asked questions of individuals. The result was that the chaos was brought to order."

People admire leaders who seem to have empathy for tough emotional situations. In one incident, an accounting clerk with a very sick family member had asked co-workers to answer her phone when she wasn't there, reported the respondent. "When they didn't, she swore and walked out. Our supervisor talked to her about her language and walking out when she was angry. He told her it wasn't appropriate, but he also let her know that he realized she was under a lot of pressure."

Sometimes the most effective response to an emotional situation is nothing more complicated than an enforced "time out." Colonel Clyde Slick, Commanding Officer of the 6th U.S. Marine Corps District, recalls the day someone taught him that lesson. "I was so angry about something I literally ran almost a mile across the base to get to my commander's office and report it," Colonel Slick remembers. "He sees me red in the face and totally angry, and says, 'Sit down, I'll be with you in just a second.' He let me sit there for over ten minutes while he did paperwork. Finally he looked up and said, 'OK, I can see you're upset. What's the problem?' Of course by that time I had calmed down considerably. Later I realized that what he did was a very intentional leadership action on his part."

On the other hand, people have little respect for leaders who sidestep difficult emotional situations. Wrote a respondent about such a leader, "He ignored complaints from subordinates. The complaints were actually requests to intervene and settle a dispute between two employees within the organization." As a result of the leader's refusal to take action, "The 'wall' or 'gap' between these two employees grew until there was an explosive outburst between them." (The question remains as to why colleagues of these employees didn't step in in true "grassroots leader" fashion. The answer may be that such situations are so challenging that people will do almost anything to avoid getting involved.)

Put Emotional Outbursts to Productive Use

The most astute grassroots leaders are able to harness the energy in emotional explosions and channel it in more productive directions. They know that where there is conflict, there is involvement and caring. Instead of trying to tamp things down, they use conflict in a positive way to get creative juices flowing. Emotional outbursts can then become starting points for significant and far-reaching results.

Respondents seem to agree that this is the stuff of advanced leadership. Said a respondent about an emotional situation between two employees, "The leader recognized the anger and hostility of the two employees, moved the discussion to a secluded area, lowered the voice levels and tone of voice, paraphrased to indicate listening, used "I" messages, became part of the problem-solving, and scheduled individual follow-up conferences. The two people began to cool off and became part of the plan for a solution—not only concerning their differences, but also the business point that they were differing on."

Another leader used a similar range of skills to turn an emotional situation around. "He handled a potentially explosive situation so that the people who were disagreeing actually became part of the solution," said the respondent. "He used 'attending' behaviors; he collected information, and then he problem-solved using the talent and skills of the two people. This resulted in a change in how one department handles its workload, a decrease in tension in the work team, and a common feeling that people are doing what they are best suited for. It was a real paradigm shift for our organization."

Grassroots Leaders Believe in Themselves

The most successful grassroots leaders in these incidents all have the confidence to enter into a test of one kind or another, usually in public, without any guarantee they will be successful. They may not necessarily be totally confident of the outcome. What they seem to have instead is enough belief in themselves to know that even if they fail, they can take it. With this faith in their own strength and ability they are able to take chances, rather than always playing it safe. Organizations are full of people who know how to play it safe. No doubt many are also credible and trustworthy people. The only trouble is, no one knows it, because no one has ever seen them show their stuff.

Grassroots Leadership Step by Step

The following tools can help you to build credibility and trust. These are described more fully in the section called "Tools: Grassroots Leadership Step by Step (pages 188–203).

Expressing Yourself: Presenting Your Thoughts and Ideas (Tool 16). The steps in this tool can help you plan a group or important one-on-one presentation and deliver your thoughts in a way that will help you achieve your purpose (pages 188–192).

Moving from Conflict to Collaboration (Tool 17). The steps in this tool help you anticipate conflict, adopt a planned approach so you can use it as an opportunity to improve communication, improve processes, build trust, and get people working together productively (pages 193–198).

Handling Emotions under Pressure (Tool 18). This tool contains seven techniques you can use to help people work through emotional situations so they can refocus their energy on the task at hand (pages 199–203).

 Credibility and trust are hard to earn, but easy to lose, and once lost, are hard to regain. This strategy is about making the right versus the expedient choice. Personal credibility and trust are revealed through a series of tests, preferably in public, in which leaders demonstrate their willingness to step up to challenging situations. Behaviors that destroy

credibility and trust include playing it safe, unethi-
cal actions, passing the buck, blaming others, and
flying off the handle. The best practices of the successful grassroots leaders are as follows:

1. They make credible presentations.
2. They do the right thing.
3. They take on tough challenges.
4. They leverage strong emotions.
5. They believe in themselves.

7

The Emotional Labor of Grassroots Leadership

THE EMOTIONAL LABOR OF GRASSROOTS LEADERSHIP: THIS CONCEPT brings all five strategies together.

Grassroots leaders today face a paradox that seems almost past resolving. On the one hand, traditional leaders have always been expected to maintain a facade of confidence and optimism. People are quick to adopt a leader's mood, after all, and the higher up the ladder the leader stands, the more people there are for him or her to affect—or infect. Why spread uncertainty, gloom, and even despair when you could be spreading confidence, optimism, and hope? On the other hand, as positional power fades in relation to personal power, today's leaders are also expected to be authentic, to share of themselves, to be *real.* This is how they build their personal credibility, which in turn is a big part of why people choose to follow them.

The critical incidents in this study make it clear that in a world in which everyone is a leader, the need to manage one's emotional state of mind is a responsibility everyone shares.

Resolving this paradox is one of the most personally difficult and even gut-wrenching aspects of leadership. What's more, if ignored, it can make everything else you do twice as difficult as it needs to be. In other words, being able to find the appropriate emotion or getting yourself into the right state of mind can mean the difference between challenging and productive leadership experiences on the one hand, and tooth-grinding, hair-tearing, emotionally draining exercises in frustration and futility on the other.

•   •   •

It's Sunday afternoon, and Nora's emotional state of mind is somewhere between homicidal and suicidal. As the product manager of a just-launched product, she knows she needs to adjust her attitude, but she doesn't want to, not just yet. She isn't ready to let go of the righteous rage that has been boiling inside her ever since she read the three e-mails from the field over the weekend. Four months of 12-hour days, and now this! The company had never gotten a product to market so quickly before—especially one with so many innovations. What's more, this product was the first one designed to meet the requirements of small distributors, along with the market served by the company's traditional sales force. Plus, Nora's team members had worked like crazy to keep costs down. More specifically, they'd stayed within the new cost-of-goods ratio that had recently been issued by the people in Finance. They'd had to stretch themselves to adapt their normal packaging design, searching out less expensive packing materials and vendors, but their determination had paid off. All in all, it was a damned good product, and she was proud of every member of the development team, from the engineers right through to the graphics people.

Now that the product was launched, she'd been expecting . . . yes, okay, a little praise from those people in the field whom she'd relied on in developing the product specs. "You did just what we asked!" would have been nice, or "Getting it done in time for the distributors' trade show made all the difference!" She was not prepared for the e-mails she got: "Why are we suddenly using such cheap packaging?" asked one salesperson. "These materials show no respect for the market," said another. Her favorite came from Sam, a very vocal and well-known distributor, part of that new group she and her team had worked so hard to please and whose requirements had dictated their backbreaking development schedule: "We can't sell this." Over the weekend, Sam had also sent along a competitor's product. "Pretty snazzy," he said, "and it costs less than ours."

Nora is furious. Why couldn't they have told her this before? How did Finance ever come up with this ridiculous cost-of-goods ratio? How big a market are these distributors, anyway? Nora drafted several blistering e-mails on Saturday. Only a recurring problem with her laptop modem prevented her from sending them out. By tomorrow, though, she has to get a grip on her emotions. Tomorrow she has to go back to her team, and together they have to pull this project out of the fire. With a word to her daughter who's on the phone in the kitchen, Nora puts on a jacket against the brisk autumn air, snaps a leash on the dog, and slips out the front door. Maybe a half-hour walk will help her get her head together.

•   •   •

The Emotional Foundations of the CLIMB Strategies

As we described in earlier chapters, there is a different emotion or state of mind for each CLIMB strategy, which successful grassroots leaders are able to adopt or tap into:

- When they create a compelling future, they call on a basic sense of optimism. Despite the obstacles or risks they foresee, they still believe, deep down, that in the long run the rewards will be worth the effort. This optimism keeps them moving forward, even when the going gets rough.

- When they let the customer drive the organization, they draw on a deep caring for customers. When customers challenge their pet ideas, or seem unreasonable or demanding, what keeps leaders going is a real appreciation of customers, their needs and dilemmas, and a strong desire to see them succeed.

- To involve every mind, leaders are patient yet persistent. When they introduce new ideas, they know it will take time for people to buy in. They keep the door open, they keep inviting people in, but they don't make any ultimatums.

- To manage work horizontally, they stay open and suspend their judgment. They try to develop loyalty to the organization as a whole, rather than only to their part of it. They're able to see the practices of other departments as different, not right or wrong. By not being judgmental, they gain the cooperation of other groups more easily; they also make life easier on themselves.

- To build personal credibility, they rely on a belief in themselves. They're willing to take risks and to admit their mistakes, because they have a fairly well-developed sense of their own worth.

What we see when we read between the lines of these critical incidents, and also when we reflect on our own experience, is that leaders who can tap into the right emotional state or adopt the right attitude for a particular strategy seem to do a better job. The work they must do seems easier and less stressful, and as a result they seem to do a better job of making their case and connecting with other people. Their efforts to create a compelling future, for example, are more fruitful, because they are able to convey their own optimism about the future, which other people naturally respond to. When trying to get a change initiative off the ground, it's easier for them to accept the inevitable setbacks that come with trying to "involve every mind," because, although they don't give up, they are prepared to be patient. And so forth.

There's nothing in our study to indicate that these grassroots leaders were born with an extra supply of these emotions or attitudes. What seems more likely is that when they need to focus on a particular strategy, they are able to exercise the appropriate emotional labor.

Emotional labor, the concept we described in Chapter 3 about customers, refers to the effort required to express those emotions that a customer consciously or unconsciously expects during a one-to-one interaction with a representative of an organization. When what the customer expects is identical or almost identical with what the employee feels, the emotional labor is minimal. The bigger the gap, the more emotional labor is required to bridge it. Customer service representatives immediately grasp this concept; emotional labor is something they practice from the minute they start their daily roller-coaster ride of wildly unpredictable customer conversations: "You never got the part we sent? I'm sorry that happened. We'll send you another one." "You're still confused about your statement? I'll be happy to go over it with you again." "You think we're a bunch of rip-off artists? Hm well, if I thought someone was cheating me, I'd be angry, too. Tell me what happened."

As far as the customer is concerned, these service providers are demonstrating appropriately professional behavior. Are they acting? Sometimes they probably are. A better question might be, "In any given interaction, how much emotional labor must they expend to make the interaction positive and productive for the customer and the organization?"

Putting Yourself in the Right Frame of Mind

People perform emotional labor every time they must make an effort to call up a smile or positive response, or resist the temptation to step in and tell somebody what to do. What seems to set successful grassroots leaders apart is that (1) they have a greater awareness of the importance of the emotional component in their work, and (2) they make more of a conscious effort to tap into or call up the emotional state that will best support and amplify whatever leadership strategy or skill they are engaged in.

As a result, they may be less likely to burn out. Rather than feeling totally overwhelmed by an inability to get a project off the ground, they understand that expending the emotional labor to be patient and persistent will, in conjunction with other behaviors, eventually produce results. Successful leaders may also find it easier to tap into whatever emotion is called for in those small moments, which the critical incidents reveal to be so impactful—in almost the same way customer service providers respond to each customer interaction they are presented with.

The real question is, how far can emotional labor take you? What can you do if you feel deficient in any one of these emotional states—either temporarily or permanently?

Unfortunately, we have no magic potion that will make you instantly optimistic, or patient, or nonjudgmental. However, if you find yourself in a situation calling for an attitude or emotion, there are some steps you can take to get a better understanding of where you stand, and to prepare for planned and unplanned leadership opportunities in ways that will maximize your areas of greatest strength.

Vent.   Get in your car, roll the windows up, turn on the radio, and scream. Complain to your spouse, or some other caring person not connected with your job.

Look inside yourself.   Chapter 2 ("Create a Compelling Future") included an interview with a woman who, when she was not feeling optimistic, would ask herself a few questions: Did she have the skills she needed? The resources? Was she simply exhausted? You can use the same approach to shed some light on problems you're having with other strategies. What's preventing you from being as patient as you need to be to involve every mind? What would it take to feel more confident about demonstrating your personal credibility?

Do some mental rehearsing.   You're about to meet with another department, whose way of working strikes you as, well, stupid. The meeting begins. Someone from the department says something that strikes you as particularly misguided. Imagine yourself saying, "Interesting. I've never thought of it in those terms. I'd be interested in your thinking on that."

Assume positive intent.   People caught up in organizational change aren't always at their best. However, if you can give them the benefit of the doubt, you'll stand a greater chance of mustering the patience, or openness, or optimism you need.

Fake it until you make it.   Feelings produce behavior. Behavior can also produce feelings. This approach is also known as *act as if.* Act patiently, in other words, and you will come to feel more patient. Try it; it works.

Overlearn.   There's a concept in skills development known as *overlearning.* It refers to the fact that when you're going to be using a skill in very challenging and unpredictable situations, you need to reach a higher-than-normal level of mastery so that when you need to perform it, you can focus on the challenging situation, rather than on how to perform the skill.

Lighten your emotional load.   There are often steps you can take to prepare for leadership situations calling for emotional responses that you know are difficult for you. If, for example, you're concerned about how optimistic you can be about a new program you need to introduce, why not get someone who's more outgoing and upbeat to help out in some way, perhaps by co-leading the meeting?

The above steps apply to all the strategies. There are also some specific things you can do to be more successful with each strategy.

- To maintain or generate the optimism you need to create a compelling future, list the reasons you have to feel optimistic, and focus on those. Don't disasterize. In other words, just because your sales were off this quarter doesn't mean your company's products are no good.

- To find the genuine caring you need to let the customer drive the organization, spend time with some customers, if you can. Learn about all their concerns and challenges, not simply those that are related to your organization. If you can't spend time with them, talk to people who do. Read about your customers; look them up on the Internet. Check out the trade journals for their business or industry. Anything you can do to appreciate their position will increase your concern for their welfare.

- To be as patient and persistent as you need to be to involve every mind, set small milestones. Reset them as necessary. If you're revisiting decisions you thought had been made, make this an interim milestone. Keep your focus on what you have accomplished.

- To maintain the openness you need to manage work horizontally, play the devil's advocate. Put yourself in the other person's shoes. Imagine how that person must be experiencing this situation.

- To develop the faith in yourself that you need to build personal credibility and trust, set yourself some small challenges. Get some small wins under your belt. Focus on things you have accomplished. Ask a friend or colleague how they see your abilities. They probably rate them higher than you do.

•   •   •

For once Nora is grateful that Monday morning commuter gridlock gives her time to think about meeting with her team. Her biggest concern is how she'll come across. She knows she needs to be upbeat and keep everyone moving forward. She needs to let the team members say what they want to say, but she can't let the meeting stall out on total negativity. What she'd really like to do is kick back and gripe right along with everybody else, but she can't afford to do that. On the other hand, she can't be too goody-goody, either, or she'll lose them completely.

By the time she gets to work, she has pretty well decided what she needs to do and the approach she will take. First of all, she needs to meet with her team, help members see this as a temporary setback, and keep the focus on the fact that the product is excellent and will generate substantial sales. Despite her present mood, she's confident about the product's quality. She is prepared for the fact that the team might not be ready to take this bigger-picture view right away, but in time she believes they will. She also needs to get Finance and Marketing together to reconsider this cost-of-goods ratio in a bigger picture. First, though, she's going to have to rein in her irritation with Finance for not taking the time to learn more about the pricing dynamics of their markets. If she can adopt a neutral—

or more neutral—point of view, she'll have a better understanding of why they made the decisions they did.

The most difficult realization she has come to, however, is that a lot of her anger is directed at herself. She was too quick to accept other people's assessment of this market—especially Sam's, who everybody seemed to think was the world's expert—and the type of product the market would find acceptable. Yes, the deadlines were impossible and it is a market she isn't all that familiar with, but she realizes that, deep down, she has had premonitions about the packaging all along. Rather than speak up, it was easier to trust Sam. After all, everyone else seemed to.

What she needs to do now is admit her mistake to her team, which she knows will already be angry with her. If she can get through that meeting with her credibility intact and the project still moving forward, or at least not dead in the water, she'll consider her performance a success.

• • •

To her great surprise, Nora was actually able to get out of the office before dark that evening. Soon she was on the freeway heading home, humming along to something on the radio. The traffic flowed. The brilliance of the autumn foliage caught in the late afternoon sun stood out against the darkening sky. All things considered, it had been a good day, although the team meeting had gotten off to a rocky start. When Peter went into his "Isn't it your job to know this stuff?" routine, she saw some heads nodding, and she felt herself starting to get defensive. So she took a deep breath and said, "You're right. I blew it." She smiled now at the reaction: it had completely taken the wind out of everybody's sails. From that point on, they were able to move beyond griping and blaming (for the most part) and concentrate on the repackaging issues at hand.

Her phone call later in the day to Finance took the wind out of *her* sails. Feeling a little as if she were back in junior high school asking Jimmy Boynton to the school dance, she actually tried out a few lines to make sure there was no edge to her voice before she called Lyndon. Her rehearsal paid off. "Oh what a shame," Lyndon had said, the very picture of cooperation. "If that ratio didn't work for you, you should have come to us. We could have looked into other pricing models. No point in saving money if nobody buys the product, right?"

She had to congratulate herself on the control she'd shown, not only with Lyndon but with her team—and with herself. Taking the time to plan things through in her head had paid off. She'd thought she would feel insincere and manipulative, but instead she ended up feeling very professional and purposeful.

She automatically eased her car over into the lane for her exit. In a few minutes I'll be home, she thought, and in a much more positive frame of mind than when I left the house this morning. She peered ahead, looking for the white church that marked the corner of her street. "There's a lesson to be learned here," she said to herself. "When that inner voice tells you something isn't right, pay attention. Be prepared to speak up and do something about it. Because if you don't, there may be no one else who will."

TOOLS

Grassroots Leadership Step By Step

In this section, you'll find a selection of tools and techniques to help you deal with the challenging leadership situations described in this book. We have selected tools that are particularly useful for each of the five CLIMB strategies. We have also included a self-evaluation that you can use to focus your own development plan.

These tools, which are drawn from AchieveGlobal's training programs, have been widely tested and have proven their worth in on-the-job applications. They were developed by Amy Avergun, Caryl Berrey, Maureen Kelly, Lucy Patel, Craig Perrin, and Julie Winkle of the AchieveGlobal Research and Development team. In addition, Ron Zemke and Chip R. Bell of Performance Resource Associates contributed to Tool 6.

Chapter 1: Because If You Don't No One Will

Tool 1: Look Inside: How Good a Leader Are You?

Chapter 2: Create a Compelling Future

Tool 2: Navigating Change
Tool 3: The Big Picture
Tool 4: How's It Going—Really?
Tool 5: Reframe It!

Chapter 3: Let the Customer Drive the Organization

Tool 6: Cycle of Service Analysis
Tool 7: TACT Process
Tool 8: Meeting Unspoken Customer Needs

Chapter 4: Involve Every Mind

Tool 9: Proactive Listening
Tool 10: Coaching—Bringing Out the Best in Others
Tool 11: Giving Recognition

Chapter 5: Manage Work Horizontally

Tool 12: Managing Your Priorities
Tool 13: Influencing for Win-Win Outcomes
Tool 14: The "Team Formation Checklist"
Tool 15: Raising Difficult Issues with Your Team

Chapter 6: Build Credibility and Trust

Tool 16: Expressing Yourself: Presenting Your Thoughts
          and Ideas
Tool 17: Moving from Conflict to Collaboration
Tool 18: Handling Emotions under Pressure

Look Inside:
How Good a Leader
Are You?

This leadership profile is based on the five CLIMB strategies. Completing this self-evaluation will give you an idea of how you rate your own performance as a leader, using the criteria that the critical-incident study showed others will use to judge you. The statements are grouped according to the five CLIMB strategies. Circle the number that best represents the extent to which you agree or disagree with each statement.

Strongly Disagree	Somewhat Agree	Strongly Agree
1	3	5

Create a compelling future.   **Agreement**

1. I link my work efforts to the
   organization's objectives.   1   2   3   4   5
2. I use the organization's core values
   to guide my decisions and action.   1   2   3   4   5

3. I help others understand their roles
   in the changing organization.   1   2   3   4   5
4. I help others develop positive
   approaches to emerging needs in the
   organization.   1   2   3   4   5
5. I help ensure that my work group or
   team undertakes appropriate planning
   activities.   1   2   3   4   5
6. I challenge assumptions that may
   keep the organization from moving
   forward.   1   2   3   4   5

Your Score _____

Let the customer drive the organization.   Agreement

7. I meet with customers or review
   customer feedback regularly.   1   2   3   4   5
8. I help ensure that timely, accurate
   customer data is gathered and
   distributed.   1   2   3   4   5
9. I make sure that people know how
   their work affects the customer.   1   2   3   4   5
10. I am always watching for ways to
    make it easier for customers to deal
    with us.   1   2   3   4   5
11. I hold my work group or team
    accountable for considering the
    customer in its decision making.   1   2   3   4   5
12. I keep informed about what the
    competition is doing to win
    customers.   1   2   3   4   5

Your Score _____

Involve every mind.   Agreement

13. I seek ideas and opinions from
    individuals throughout the
    organization.   1   2   3   4   5
14. I help ensure that people are involved
    in decisions that affect their work.   1   2   3   4   5

15. I encourage people to speak up when
    they disagree.   1 2 3 4 5
16. I involve all relevant stakeholders
    when engaging in problem solving.   1 2 3 4 5
17. I help others learn and grow by
    providing feedback, coaching, and/
    or training.   1 2 3 4 5
18. I seek opportunities to recognize
    others' contributions.   1 2 3 4 5

Your Score _____

Manage work horizontally.   Agreement

19. I look for ways to build teamwork
    within and across work groups.   1 2 3 4 5
20. I challenge unnecessary barriers
    (policies, procedures, etc.) to working
    across functions.   1 2 3 4 5
21. I apply my technical expertise to help
    solve problems related to cross-
    functional work.   1 2 3 4 5
22. I help track progress toward
    improvement of cross-functional
    work processes.   1 2 3 4 5
23. I help plan and implement cross-
    functional projects.   1 2 3 4 5
24. I help ensure that my work group or
    team meets deadlines that affect the
    work of other functions.   1 2 3 4 5

Your Score _____

Build personal credibility.   Agreement

25. I consistently treat others with honesty
    and respect.   1 2 3 4 5
26. I admit when I've made a mistake.   1 2 3 4 5
27. I confront issues with others directly
    rather than avoid problems or go
    around them.   1 2 3 4 5
28. I actively seek feedback regarding my
    strengths and weaknesses.   1 2 3 4 5

29. I model the behaviors that I expect
    others to practice.   1   2   3   4   5
30. I seize opportunities for personal
    growth and learning.   1   2   3   4   5

                        Your Score _____

Interpreting Your Scores

Although your scores represent your evaluation of your own
leadership, they are based on the criteria that others use to
judge you. A lower score for a particular strategy indicates you
may want to spend some time reviewing the competencies on
which that strategy is based.

2

Navigating Change

Whether your change initiative is organization-wide or limited to a single facility, function, or team, the techniques of "Navigating Change" can help you and others achieve the desired results.

You can move toward becoming a navigator of change by taking the steps outlined in this tool. Decide the particular change you will focus on. Then answer the questions that relate to each of the four basic steps for "Navigating Change."

Step 1. Acknowledge your own reactions.

On your own or with a trusted associate, examine how you feel and what you think about the change. Be honest. You might also list pros and cons in writing. Ask yourself:

  A. How do you feel about this change?
     Don't "fix" it if it's not broken.

B. What concerns, if any, do you have about this change?
Do the execs really know what our customers need from us? Have they done the research? It doesn't seem so.

Step 2. Assess the Impact of the Change.

Gather information and talk to as many people as possible to get a variety of perspectives on what the effects of the change will be. Assemble your information; use an outline, list, drawing, or flowchart. Summarize the information to help you evaluate the change. Answer these questions:

A. What aspects of the change do you need to have clarified?
How will we track the effects on our customers?

B. What might happen if this change isn't made now?
We may not be able to keep our prices competitive.

C. What are some positive outcomes for the organization?
A more competitive service that's accessible to more markets.

D. What are some positive outcomes for you?
A chance to make some long-needed changes in how we handle service renewals.

E. How does this change affect you? Your work group? Other groups you interact with?
More work and confusion at first, but then some real improvements if we can hold everything together through the changeover process.

F. What's hard about this change?
Not being able to verify the information I'm getting.

Step 3. Seek and acknowledge others' reactions.

Ask people affected by the change to share their concerns or opinions. Listen and be supportive. Focus on these questions:

A. How might other people who are affected by this change feel about it?

Make a list of people's names along with their concerns. For example:

John: Resentful that he'll have to reorganize his team

Luanne: Stressed by the extra work she expects to land on her desk

Rachel: All for it because she won't be reporting to Luanne anymore

Matt: Worried that he won't have a job after the service levels change

B. What are some things you can do to acknowledge these people's feelings?

Listen, admit there are still gaps, and share my own concerns.

Step 4. Take positive action individually and with others.

After assessing your role, responsibility, and level of involvement in the change, consider:

A. Which of these activities is appropriate for you to take?

- Inform others about the change.
- Collaborate with others in implementing the change.
- Stay abreast of what's happening.
- Adjust your work to respond to the change.

B. What specific actions can you take individually? When can you do each one?

Contact Mark for answers to my coworkers' questions and my own—by March 1.

Draft a list of unresolved issues to present at the next team meeting—by March 10.

The Big Picture

This tool helps you develop a brief statement that succinctly encapsulates your organization's vision or purpose, and how your department or team fits into this larger picture. Once you have prepared this statement, you'll be surprised at how many times you'll use it: when making formal presentations, giving progress reports, answering questions, and in casual conversations with others inside or outside your group or organization.

To prepare one or more *big picture* statements, answer the four questions below. Then, using these answers, write a personalized big-picture statement that sums up what the organization (or your business unit) wants to accomplish and how your work group or team fits in. Keep your statement simple and worded in a way that is meaningful to your team.

Step 1. What are the most urgent external pressures facing the larger organization today?

Possible answers include changes in competition, customer expectations, markets, demographics, technology, regulations, and so forth. Talk with others to expand your view.

We're losing market share because we no longer have a way to differentiate our products from others available.

Step 2. What is the larger organization trying to accomplish?

For example, what is its stated vision, mission, strategy, or direction? What are its business goals and plans?

The organization's goal is to recapture its 40-percent market share and then grow that to 50 percent within two years. Its vision is to support its products with the fastest, most responsive, and personal customer service in the industry. To do that, it is installing new service desk software and reorganizing its sales and service representatives to improve communication and coordination.

Step 3. What measures of indicators are being used to track and evaluate the larger organization's progress toward its goals?

We're using customer surveys, industry statistics, and quarterly sales figures for new, repeat, and returning customers.

Step 4. In what ways does your work group or team—or you as an individual—currently contribute to what the organization is trying to accomplish?

My group is responsible for recommending the service desk software and then overseeing its installation and integration with existing systems.

At this point, it can be helpful to share your answers to questions 1 through 4 with associates who can help you clarify your understanding of the big picture. Once you are comfortable with the accuracy and depth of your answers, write a big picture statement you can use with your work group or team. Frame your statement in words that reflect the team's role and perspective.

The helpdesk software we recommend and how we manage its installation will help us reach our service goals and help regain our company's market share.

TOOL

4

How's It Going— Really?

No one has time for lengthy meetings any more. Besides, people are reluctant to reveal too much in a public setting. This tool helps you take advantage of those brief moments—in the hall, on an elevator—to find out how someone is coming along. Chances are the information you'll get will be more reliable and also more timely. What's more, because this tool is so brief, you're likely to use it more often.

Using this tool involves being alert to informal opportunities to ask coworkers, "How's it going?" Anytime that you and your team members and/or coworkers have a few minutes to exchange information can be turned into a progress check. The key is to avoid coming on as the expert with all the answers. That kind of approach risks alienating someone and may result in your unwanted ownership of the other person's issue.

Step 1. Ask how things are going.

Your aim is to find out what is on someone's mind, so the best approach is to be light and open-ended. Helpful questions begin with phrases like "What's happening with . . . ?" or "What did you find out about . . . ?"

If a person mentions several issues, focus the conversation on the one concern that the person seems most interested in or concerned about.

Step 2. Listen to the response.

Take time to tune in to the need behind the words.

- A. *I revised the manual so that everybody's finally satisfied.* (possible need: recognition from you)
- B. *I'm off to meet with Ben. Wish me luck!* (possible need: a brief coaching tip)
- C. *Jan and I decided that doing a timeline this early doesn't make sense.* (possible need: information)
- D. *Frankly, I'm stuck on this research project. I don't know what to do next.* (possible need: help weighing pros and cons)

Step 3. Ask questions to clarify the situation.

Phrase your questions carefully so they don't pressure the person or imply a negative reaction.

- A. *Wow! Even the southern region is happy with the manual?*
- B. *Why do you need luck with Ben?*
- C. *Have you and Jan talked about postponing the timeline?*
- D. *What databases have you looked at so far?*

Step 4. Respond briefly, being careful to take your cue from the other person.

Offer support, help, or information as needed.

- A. *Congratulations! They're a tough group to please!*
- B. *With Ben, I always try to give him plenty of time*

before getting back to me with an answer. He doesn't like feeling rushed.

C. *Allen told me yesterday that under the new guidelines, he can't allocate any funds without a timeline, not even for preapproved expenditures.*

D. *You know, Craig was doing similar research in the Tampa office. You might want to check with him.*

Step 5. End on a positive and productive note.

A. *You know, this manual is going to give us another way to make sure we really are a customer-driven company.*

B. *Ben's got even more to think about right now than the rest of us. But I know he will want to help out.*

C. *Allen probably has ideas for helping you remove some of the obstacles that are getting in the way of your timeline. Have you talked with him?*

D. *With the progress you've made so far, I'm confident that with more information, you'll be able to decide what needs to happen next.*

Reframe It!

This tool provides a step by step process to help someone who is frustrated with a change look at the situation in a different, more positive way. Without telling someone what to do or think, you suggest a point of view that helps the other person make choices to support the goal or strategy. Use reframing when you discover that someone is:

- Resisting a change or having trouble coping with a change
- Viewing a situation or person negatively; placing blame
- Resisting the need to question and rethink his or her assumptions
- Forgetting to experiment with new ways of thinking
- Having difficulty envisioning what's possible
- Juggling priorities or having trouble making a decision

To reframe it, take three simple steps to encourage people to find their own solutions.

Step 1. Anticipate situations in which reframing might be helpful.

Formal planning and review meetings offer opportunities, as do individual meetings with people who are having trouble understanding or agreeing with a goal or strategy.

Step 2. Offer your reframing statement.

Make statements to change a person's view of the situation. Introduce new elements, question assumptions, tell personal stories, or raise related issues. Reframing statements tend to begin with phrases like:

"Think of it as . . ."

"On the other hand . . ."

"Another way to look at it might be . . ."

"It helps me to put myself in the customer's shoes and . . ."

Be clear and brief. Elaborate only if the other person seems not to understand. Here are some examples:

Problem: "It's obvious which format works best. Why waste time debating with the other departments?"

Reframe: "On the other hand, this is the first joint decision to be made by three departments that are in the process of trying to merge."

Problem: "Why should I have to help Charlie with that project? It's not my job, and besides, I don't know anything about bookstores."

Reframe: "Another way to look at it might be that the conference bookstore is a revenue-generating activity, and we're behind this quarter."

Problem: "Spending that kind of money on TV advertising every month seems like a waste."

Reframe: "On the other hand, if our competitors are doing it, do we really have a choice?"

Step 3. Move on without demanding a response.

Some people need time to think about what you have said. Don't press for immediate agreement.

Cycle of Service Analysis

Use this tool to analyze how you are currently delivering a service. It will allow you to enhance the process to improve the customer's experience or to remove or minimize those points at which service fails to produce the desired experience.

The main benefit of analyzing and improving a cycle of service is simple: When a service experience matches or exceeds a customer's expectation, the customer usually forms a positive opinion of the organization.

Step 1. Isolate the moments of truth that satisfy a specific customer need.

A *moment of truth** occurs any time a customer comes in contact with your organization and uses that opportunity to judge the quality of your service. A *cycle of service** is a series of

---

* The "Moments of Truth" and "Cycle of Service" analysis techniques were pioneered by our partners, Ron Zemke and Chip Bell, of Performance Research Associates in the late 1980s.

moments of truth that a customer experiences from the beginning to the end of a service interaction (from a customer's recognition of a need to the satisfaction of that need). Figure T6.1 illustrates a cycle of service, in which the black dots represent moments of truth.

For example, when you go to a restaurant, you might experience the following moments of truth: park the car, enter the restaurant, ask for a table, wait, walk to the table, wait, order a drink, wait, order food, wait, eat, ask for your check, wait, pay the check, and leave. By describing that cycle of service and examining each moment of truth, the restaurant manager can identify both potential fail points and opportunities to enhance your experience.

A telephone company, for instance, has distinct cycles of service: initiating service, getting a bill, and getting the phone repaired. An airline also has clear cycles: making a reservation, checking in, boarding, eating, claiming baggage, and so on. When you identify the moments of truth in a cycle, you begin to see service from the point of view of your customer, who ultimately determines if a need is well or poorly met.

Figure T6.1 Cycle of service. The black dots represent moments of truth.

Step 2. Identify the moments with the greatest impact on the customer's experience—the *key* moments of truth.

In a cycle with many key moments, you might ask:

- Which moments affect the greatest number of customers?
- Which moments are likely to cause the most irritation?
- Which moments, if improved, could save money or improve profits?
- Which moments could be improved at minimal cost?
- Which moments can we improve without help from other departments?

Step 3. Identify enhancers, detractors, solutions, and minimizers for each moment of truth.

If the moment is now meeting expectation, look for ways to enhance the experience. These *enhancers* might make the experience easier, faster, or better in some other way. Enhancers express your service strategy in ways that your customers will notice and appreciate.

Take special note of *detractors*—a filled parking lot, confusing signs, misinformation, delays, rudeness, and so on. Sometimes the fix is simple and immediate—replacing pens in a bank, for example, before they run out of ink.

Consider whether to use a *minimizer.* Some detractors, often the result of unfriendly systems or rules, require long-term solutions. So improving the customer's experience right now may call for a minimizer to give you time to address the underlying problem. For example, bank customers might say they're unhappy about long lines in the lobby. You may not be able to shorten the wait, but you might reduce the pain with a number system or something for the customers to read or watch.

Step 4. Confirm and clarify the moments of truth by communicating directly with customers.

Cycle of service analysis, grounded in feedback from customers and service providers, is a vital tool for improving your customer's service experience.

TACT Process

The TACT process is useful during a service interaction whenever one of the following customer-related issues may be causing difficulty or confusion:

Physical/sensory issues, such as a visible disability

Technology issues, such as confusion about technology-related instructions

Language issues, such as difficulty understanding your words

Differing expectations, such as what constitutes good service

The key to the process is, of course, *tact*—that is, meeting the customer's business need without offending the customer. The letters T-A-C-T represent the four steps in the TACT process.

Step 1. Take note of cues.

Before asking questions or taking action, it's important to confirm that one of the four issues may be involved (physical/sensory, language, technology, or differing expectations). Start with your understanding of the customer's business goal. Then look for direct and indirect cues that may point to one of the four issues. Keep in mind that some cues may indicate a range of issues:

Physical/sensory issues.   A visible disability, a physical aid (a cane, for example), difficulty performing a task, reluctance to perform a task, difficulty reading, difficulty understanding your words, your difficulty understanding the customer's words

Technology issues.   Reluctance to operate a device, frustration with a device, confusion about technology-related instructions, inability to interpret computer-generated information

Language issues (both oral and written).   Difficulty understanding your words, your difficulty understanding the customer's words, difficulty reading, reluctance to read or write in your presence

Differing expectations.   A visible difference in general appearance, unexpected behaviors (for instance, lack of eye contact or a differing sense of personal space), unwillingness to follow standard procedures, difficulty understanding your words, your difficulty understanding the customer's words

While noting cues, maintain a pleasant manner and avoid hasty conclusions.

Step 2. Ask respectful questions.

Respectful questions help you interpret cues and better understand the issue involved (physical/sensory, language, technology, or differing expectations). They also allow the customer to volunteer a preferred way to handle the issue. You might ask:

What can I do to be more clear?
How would you like me to help?
Is there a next step that would make you more comfortable?

Would you be willing to suggest another approach?
Is there any other information that would help me meet
your needs?

It's usually best to avoid naming the issue with a question like "Are you having a problem with the ATM?" An alternative question like "May I be of any assistance?" causes no discomfort and allows the customer to suggest a next step. Where possible, follow the customer's lead in mentioning or not mentioning the issue. In summary, a respectful question:

Maintains the customer's self-esteem

Focuses on the customer's business goal

Gives the customer a chance to make a suggestion

Doesn't call undue attention to the issue involved

Step 3. Consider options.

Considering options gives you and your customer a chance to find a solution that works for the organization and the customer. Asking questions often leads to a discussion of the customer's preferred option. Think about the trade-offs involved: Does it meet the needs of the organization as well as the customer? If it does, take appropriate action. If it doesn't, tactfully explain the situation and suggest an alternative. For example:

I'm sorry we can't allow your daughter to help you read
the written driving test. The test is designed to measure
your own knowledge of the vehicle code. However, we do
have the same test in three other languages.

After the customer responds to your suggestion, ask further respectful questions and consider further options as necessary.

Step 4. Take appropriate action.

With this step, you carry out the option that you and the customer have agreed to. As you take action, remain alert to cues that the option is or isn't working for the customer, and continue to respect the customer's need for dignity.

At this moment of truth, only the customer can determine if

your action is appropriate. If there's any question in your mind, confirm by asking respectfully if the option is appropriate. It's especially important to ask permission if the option involves physically touching the customer or a physical aid, such as a wheelchair.

With language issues, be sure to confirm what you will do. You might say, for example, "All right then. I'll give you this form in Spanish, and your signature goes in the dark areas on each page."

If the option proves inappropriate or inadequate, ask further respectful questions, and look for other acceptable options.

Meeting Unspoken Customer Needs

Use this tool to find and meet an unspoken customer need by doing something thrifty, rapid, on-target, and impressive. This tool is a method for meeting unspoken customer needs. Most of your work, though, involves meeting a stated need—a need that the customer actually tells you about. An auto repair shop customer, for example, might need an oil change. That is the stated need. However, this customer might also have an unspoken need: a waiting room, a cup of coffee, something to read, or a ride to and from work.

So, when is the right time to find and meet an unspoken need? Any time you're responding to a stated customer need.

Step 1. Look and listen for cues.

Listen beyond the words and read between the lines. Observe expressions, gestures, voice tone, words, and props. Watch for emotional indicators. In general, open yourself to all the cues that may indicate an unspoken customer need.

Words and voice.   The tone of voice and the specific vocabulary can tell you about unspoken customer needs. For example, a questioning tone may mean that the customer needs reassurance or assistance. Here are some examples:

"Can anyone access this data?" spoken in a hushed voice might indicate that the customer needs reassurance about security.

"Hey, which option would you choose?" in a friendly tone might show you that the customer wants a personal connection with someone in the organization.

Body language.   Posture, gestures, and facial expressions offer a wealth of information. Consider the difference in meaning when the words "That was helpful" are coupled with a sarcastic facial expression versus an open smile. Even without words, body language can provide insight to the customer's frame of mind.

Stiff posture and a rigid facial expression could mean that the customer feels uncomfortable, is emotionally distressed, or isn't naturally very expressive. When facial expressions seem at odds with what the person is saying (for instance, when a customer says, "I'm fine," while clearly expressing anger), you have the opportunity to look for unspoken needs.

Appearance and props.   It's all too easy to generalize about people by how they dress. Nevertheless, clothes, accessories, and general appearance can give you additional hints about the customer's unspoken needs. Some common props include wireless phone, clothing, shoes, pager, personal computer, tool belt, briefcase, jewelry, automobile, hat, and so forth.

Context.   Events that seem perfectly normal in one context can take on a different meaning in another setting. For instance, if one customer usually contacts the organization during daytime business hours, what might it mean if she calls with an urgent request at 4:00 A.M.? Time and place are the two main indicators of context. Here are some samples of context cues:

The customer calls at a different time, uses a service for the first time after a long history of not using that service, or contacts the organization from an unexpected location.

Step 2. Review relevant data.

Remember any past encounter with this customer and customers who might have had similar unspoken needs. Retrieve relevant information from any available sources. Add this relevant information to present cues to identify unspoken needs. Adding to the cues you can see or hear, other relevant data can help you identify unspoken customer needs. Useful information can be found from almost any source:

- Personal recollections of interactions with the customer
- Coworkers' recollections of interactions with the customer
- Customer profiles in computer databases
- Your knowledge of customers with similar profiles
- Paper files on the customer or the account
- Notes, telephone messages, and memos related to the customer
- News clippings related to the customer
- Your knowledge of customers with similar profiles
- Market research
- General information about the area
- Services the customer may not know are available

Step 3. Ask for more effective and sensitive questions from the customer to uncover additional cues and confirm your hunch.

Step 4. Improvise to impress.

Be creative. Be dramatic. Think outside the box. Think about both immediate and long-term effects. Take a calculated risk, but balance the costs with the rewards.

Step 5. Reflect, record, and share.

Think through what you've done and what happened as a result. Make note of any useful information for you and your coworkers in future interactions with this customer. Share information with coworkers about this customer, about something you've done that could be also done for other customers, and about the pitfalls of the action you've taken.

9

Proactive Listening

This tool provides a series of specific steps for improving your listening habits and managing and focusing conversations. The techniques are especially helpful when you have to deal with complex and emotionally charged issues, and when you are dealing with people whose ways of relating to others is different from yours.

Step 1. Show Interest in what the speaker has to say.

Focus on the speaker. On average, people think four times faster than they speak. Your mind's ability to race ahead of the speaker can lead to daydreaming and other distracting listening behaviors. Clear your mind of other things and use the time to say to yourself, "I need to listen to this." Concentrate on thinking about how the content:

- Connects to what you already know
- Applies to your current work
- Affects future projects and endeavors

If you're unable to focus on the speaker due to competing demands for your time and attention, be candid and defer the conversation to a specified time in the future.

Openly tell the speaker that you are interested, and why. Letting the speaker know specifically why you are interested encourages communication and also focuses the conversation.

> *I know you've been involved with these issues for a long time, so I'm very interested in hearing your viewpoint.*

> *I understand you have a rather different perspective on this issue than Mike does. Will you tell me how you see it?*

> *You look upset. Tell me what happened at the meeting.*

Use nonverbal cues to establish and maintain rapport. For example:

- Face the speaker and lean forward.
- Maintain open body language.
- Establish eye contact.
- Nod and smile when appropriate.
- Allow time for the speaker to respond or elaborate.

When the speaker pauses or hesitates, use short verbal cues to encourage continued communication. Verbal cues such as "uh-huh," "mmm," "I see," "okay," and "I understand" help you remain engaged in the conversation and help the speaker feel comfortable sharing more information. Other examples:

> *Tell me more.*

> *This is great information for me.*

Avoid interrupting the speaker with your own experiences, ideas, or opinions. Inserting your own thoughts can be tempting, but it instantly shifts the focus from the speaker to you. If you really want to draw the speaker out and receive all the information you can, avoid interrupting except to clarify and encourage. Let the speaker finish before making your own points.

Step 2. Ask questions to clarify, gather information, and focus the conversation.

Use open-ended questions to probe for more information. Open-ended questions encourage the speaker to explain, expand, describe, explore, or elaborate. They begin with words such as *what, how, tell me, describe,* and *explain.* Although *why* and *how* also begin open-ended questions, use them sparingly because they tend to put the speaker on the defensive. Use open-ended questions when:

- You see that the speaker is uncommunicative or reluctant.
- You want to stimulate conversation.
- You need to understand the big picture.
- You need a broad range of responses.
- You're not certain exactly what information you need.
- You need to bring out the other person's concerns, ideas, or feelings.
- You're trying to build involvement, trust, or rapport.
- You want to promote self-discovery.
- You need to clarify points you aren't sure you understand.

For example:

What's your view of the situation?

Tell me what the current thinking is in operations.

Limit the use of closed-ended questions. Closed-ended questions often begin with words such as *can, do, is,* or *will.* By design, they tend to limit responses—usually to a yes, a no, or a simple fact. Although these questions limit communication, they can be effective when you want to narrow the discussion or pinpoint specific information. Consider using closed-ended questions when:

- You need to direct the conversation to a specific topic or issue.
- You are certain of the facts you will need.

- Your time is limited.
- You see that the speaker is rambling.
- You want to verify information or confirm your understanding.
- You want to confirm the speaker's support, commitment, or agreement.

For example:

Is the project currently on schedule?

Can we fill this order by Tuesday?

Will your group take responsibility for this?

If necessary, use questions to manage the conversation. Questions can help you manage a conversation that may have gone off on a tangent or may be going on too long. A well-structured, open-ended question can help refocus the speaker on key points. A closed-ended question can help bring closure when a conversation has reached its conclusion.

That's interesting, but let's go back to the point you were making about the line. What exactly do you think is the source of the bottleneck? So, do you feel like we have a workable solution here?

Step 3. Let the speaker know what you understand.

Restate in your own words what you've heard. When there is a logical break in the conversation, paraphrase or summarize what you have heard. This gives the speaker the opportunity to correct or clarify.

So, the whole deal is dependent on whether or not state funding comes through.

It sounds like you are not getting the support you need from the other members of the team.

In other words, their hot button is not price, but service.

If the speaker does not agree with your restatement, try again until you have a match.

So, it's not a matter of whether the state funds come through, but rather when they are available.

Oh, I get it, both price and service are hot buttons.

Acknowledge the speaker's emotions. This will make the speaker feel accepted and will help him or her work through the emotions and get to the point.

You sound pretty fed up with the situation.

That must have been terribly disappointing.

I can understand your reluctance.

Coaching—Bringing Out the Best in Others

This tool helps you to recognize coaching opportunities, plan a coaching session, and offer your coaching in a way that doesn't sound as if you're giving orders. Consider coaching when someone:

- Asks you for advice, assistance, feedback, or support
- Is taking on a new task or responsibility
- Appears frustrated or confused
- Seems indecisive or stuck
- Is performing inconsistently
- Expresses a desire to improve
- Performs below acceptable standards
- Has a negative attitude that is impeding work

It's also important to know when *not* to coach. The following situations are probably not good coaching opportunities:

- You don't have a relationship of mutual respect and trust with the person.
- You are angry about the situation.
- The person is very busy or under deadline pressure.

Step 1. Identify an opportunity to help someone expand on his or her skills, knowledge, and abilities.

Look for signals or cues indicating that coaching could add value.

Step 2. Confirm that the person is ready for coaching.

Ask straightforward questions to gauge the person's readiness and interest.

Would you be interested in talking about what happened?

Do you have a few minutes to discuss this further?

Step 3. Ask questions to clarify the situation.

Begin each question with words like what, when, where, who, or how much. Use how and why sparingly because they tend to put people on the defensive.

How much progress has been made so far?

What happened as a result?

Frame questions that will draw out facts. Avoid threatening questions that might evoke a defensive reaction.

Why did you do that? (threatening question)

What factors led to that decision? (nonthreatening question)

Ask questions to build awareness, not to solve the problem. To accomplish this, all you need to know is that the person has the right information to move ahead.

Step 4. Offer information as appropriate.

Offer only necessary information, providing whatever the person needs to choose a course of action. How much information you offer will depend on the situation. To help someone learn a technical procedure, you might have to give quite a bit of detailed information. To help someone think of a creative solution, you might need to give less.

Listen carefully. Don't interrupt with your own ideas. Pay attention to both the facts and the train of thought, reserving all comments until the person completes a point. If the person wanders from the topic, ask a question to refocus on the issue. This keeps both you and the person you are coaching on track, but it still allows the person to lead the discussion.

Could you explain how that point relates to the main topic—the rationale behind the coding system?

If necessary, take brief notes. From time to time, summarize what you've heard.

Let's make sure I'm following. You've called the graphic artist, found the logo ideas he submitted last year, and shown them to the PR firm.

Step 5. Help the person identify possible actions.

Ask questions to help the person generate a list of possible actions.

What steps could you take to reduce the confusion about these codes?

If you could do anything that you wanted about the new packaging in the next two weeks, what would it be?

Avoid offering your own ideas until after the person you're coaching has finished.

Encourage thinking aloud, and ask for far-fetched as well as practical ideas. List ideas without commenting on their feasibility.

What other actions can you think of? They don't have to be the typical things we do around here.

Help the person identify false, negative, or inhibiting beliefs. Beliefs about how things must be done often make it difficult to generate creative solutions.

What if we didn't need different packaging for each of our products? Then would you approach the problem differently?

Help the person weigh the pros and cons of each option.

Let's look at the arguments for and against each of these options. What are the benefits of forming a task force? What are the drawbacks?

Step 6. Gain agreement on a course of action.

Ask questions to prompt the person to make firm decisions. Avoid asking "What do you think you'll do?" Instead, ask:

What are you going to do?

If the person identifies several possible actions, follow up with a question like:

Which of these alternatives will you put into action?

Ask further questions to clarify the plan.

When will you do that?
Will this option address the immediate problem?
What obstacles might you have to deal with?
Who needs to know about your plan?

Be sure to address the person's need for support.

What kind of support will you need?
How and when will you get this support?

Conclude with an open-ended question to bring out any lingering doubts and to be sure that nothing is omitted.

What other concerns do you want to discuss?

Step 7. Offer your support.

Be ready to give additional help if and when it's needed. End on a positive note by expressing your continued interest and your confidence in the person.

I've seen you handle glitches like this many times. As you get into this one, I'll be available if you want to talk. Let me know if you need a friendly ear.

Giving Recognition

This tool helps you identify behaviors you want to reinforce, and to provide a series of steps you can take when giving recognition to make sure the exchange feels comfortable and achieves its intended impact.

Step 1. Identify an opportunity for giving recognition.

Ask yourself which behaviors and actions add value to your work group and help your organization meet its business goals.

Look for group as well as individual contributions. Group accomplishments can sometimes get lost as you look for individual achievements. Some people's contributions to the group effort may be more obvious than those of others, so it's important to also recognize the group as a whole and to encourage all group members to share the credit. Be on the alert for opportunities to give recognition when you see the following behaviors:

- Taking the customer's point of view
- Working collaboratively with people in other functions

- Communicating necessary information to others in a clear and timely manner
- Analyzing work processes to simplify them or to eliminate waste and repetition
- Questioning whether the way things have always been done is necessarily the best way
- Learning new skills
- Staying abreast of what's happening in the organization and industry, and sharing that information with the rest of the group
- Taking initiative to solve problems
- Accomplishing a step that contributes to the end goal

Determine an appropriate method and form of recognition. If you avoid a "cookie-cutter" approach to giving recognition and, instead, consider the individuals you are dealing with, your recognition will be more effective. Observe the people you work with and think about what would motivate them. Consider the following:

- Will they respond well to recognition in front of others, or would a one-on-one conversation, voice mail, e-mail, or a memo make them more comfortable?
- Will praise alone be enough, or should you underscore your praise with some other form of recognition?
- What other forms of recognition would appeal to them? (Consider their interests and hobbies, what they do with their leisure time, and to what they aspire in their career development.)

Step 2. State how the behavior made a difference to you and to the organization.

When you meet with the person or group, point out why the behavior is important to the organization and to you. Identify the payoffs.

Pamela, the new assembly process you suggested will cut our costs by 50 percent in the first year alone. It was a terrific idea.

Congratulations to everyone on the task force! The new assembly process you came up with will save us thousands of dollars in the first six months alone.

If appropriate, offer some concrete form of recognition. Though praise alone is a strong motivator, backing it up with some concrete form of recognition can multiply the effects. The form of recognition you offer may be as simple and cost-free as a thank-you note placed on the person's office door or as expensive as a gift certificate or a special dinner. If you've done your homework in Step 1, you will be able to offer something that appeals to the individual or group you're recognizing. However, offering a concrete form of recognition doesn't replace the need for using Steps 1 and 2—it simply underscores your sincerity.

If appropriate, reaffirm your recognition and offer your support. This is particularly important if the behavior you are recognizing involved taking risks or trying out new ways of doing things.

Marge, if you'd like help putting your presentation together next time you have an idea like that, just let me know. I'll make sure you can get access to the chart copier, too.

If the person you are recognizing tries to deflect your praise, respond by briefly restating your recognition.

Kevin, I know you think you're just doing your job, but it's how you're doing it that's special. Rejects are down because of your ideas, and that's making a big difference.

Step 3. Describe the behavior as immediately and as specifically as possible.

Mention important details such as when the behavior occurred and what issue or problem it addressed. Avoid generalizations. Be specific and descriptive. Whenever possible, include information about when and how much.

INEFFECTIVE	EFFECTIVE
That was a great job this morning.	*I really liked the way you supported Julie during the presentation when she needed more data to make her case.*
I liked your report.	*Your report was very thorough, especially the way you described the overseas markets and correlated sales to the survey we did on customer satisfaction.*

Don't undercut praise with criticism. Don't dilute your recognition of positive behaviors by adding a critical follow-up comment or by sandwiching praise between negative remarks. Such critical comments cancel out the effects of your praise because people tend to focus on negative statements. That's exactly what you don't want to have happen when your intention is to reinforce the positive.

12

Managing Your Priorities

When you are managing work horizontally you will be faced with many conflicting demands on your time. This tool includes three interpersonal techniques that help you manage your priorities and communicate your needs clearly to others. "Learn More" focuses on how to clarify expectations for a task that is delegated to you. "Ask for Help" provides ways to cope when you are overloaded. "Give It Away" shows you how to hand off a task to someone else.

Learn More

Use this technique when you need to clarify a new assignment, when you are unclear what's expected of you, or when you need to gain a broader perspective on a problem. Once you decide who is the best person to provide the information you need, meet with that person and follow these six steps.

1. Determine how the task fits into the larger picture. Asking how the task affects business and the organization

as a whole will help you understand the importance of the task and identify the most critical aspects.

2. Ask about the main results and the standards required. Along with probing to understand the major results expected of you, be sure to find out if there are specific standards for measuring your performance.

3. Agree on the roles and responsibilities of each person. Make sure you know what authority you have and under what circumstances you should seek advice or assistance.

4. Pinpoint the required resources. Resources can be a source of conflict down the line. It is critical to flush out issues up front. If appropriate, it may be advisable to ask the other person to obtain resources that may be hard to secure—or to ask how to obtain them yourself.

5. Review key points to be sure you understand. When you take on a task, it is easy for misunderstandings to arise. Recapping the information you obtain will reduce time spent later to resolve problems.

6. Suggest a date for an early progress review. Most tasks are a series of small steps. An early progress review before you've gone too far will ensure that you're going in the right direction.

Ask for Help

Use this technique when you need to negotiate schedules or resources, or when you are overloaded.

If asking for help is new or uncomfortable for you, it's best to prepare what you'll say before you meet with others to discuss solutions. With this technique, you show you have considered the situation carefully and are not overreacting.

Before the Meeting

1. Analyze your current situation. When you feel overwhelmed or under deadline pressure, it's not easy to focus on concrete issues. Step back and do some thinking and assessing on your own. List commitments and deadlines. Assemble relevant documents such as project time-

lines and checklists. Think through how you want to present your situation.

2. List some alternatives. Consider all the alternatives. They may include reordering priorities, postponing a deadline, shifting responsibility to someone in a better position to assume it, or hiring temporary help. List those that seem most workable and be prepared to discuss the pros and cons of each.

3. Request a meeting with the appropriate people. Depending on your situation, you may need to meet with one or more persons. In some cases, you will need to talk to your manager or work-group leader. In others, you may need to talk to a coworker or to other members of your team.

At the Meeting

4. Explain the situation. In your description, focus on one or two difficulties. Emphasize your concerns about maintaining quality and mention the potential effect on customers, if that is a factor. Use objective, neutral language to describe what is happening or may happen. For example, you might say:

To attend this conference, I need to postpone my meeting with Interscan. Because they're eager to find a vendor as soon as possible, a delay like this might cost us the contract.

The deadline for the tracking system was moved up a month, and I'm still learning the software. I'm concerned that if I move ahead with this project, I'll fall behind on my regular commitments.

The schedule is so tight that it doesn't allow for mistakes or problems with the equipment.

5. Discuss possible solutions. Present the alternatives you listed and listen to other suggestions with an open mind. Weigh the pros and cons of each idea and arrive at a mutually agreeable solution. Even if you are not completely comfortable with the solution, you will be in a better position for having made your concerns known.

Give It Away

If you are deliberating about whether to delegate or hand off a task, ask yourself these questions:

- Is this task keeping me from getting to my high-priority tasks?
- Is this a task that someone else could master quickly?
- Are there others (inside or outside the organization) who are qualified and available to take on this task?
- Is there time to explain the task and its objectives adequately and still allow for its execution?

If the task is recurring and you conclude that you want to delegate it, but can't right now because there are no qualified people available, try an interim approach:

- Identify and line up prospective people immediately.
- Review the task with an eye to breaking it down into its parts so you can delegate a piece of it as soon as possible.

When you are ready to delegate a task, review the steps below to prepare for a meeting with the other person. Then use the steps during your discussion.

1. Describe the task and its place in the larger picture. Begin with a brief description of why the task is important. Help the person see how the task affects the quality of the final product. You may also want to explain why it is an appropriate task for this person to take on.

2. Work with the person to clarify the major results and standards required. Give the person a clear statement of the outcome you expect and when you expect it. A fuzzy picture can lead to frustration and misdirected energy. For most tasks, you can leave the *how-to* up to the person doing the work.

3. Agree on the roles and responsibilities of each person. In general, grant as much authority and leeway in decision making as possible. Doing so will increase the person's motivation and commitment to the task. If you have to set

limits (such as the time allowed or the kinds of decisions that must be referred to others), state them clearly.

4. Pinpoint the required resources. Describe the resources you can provide. Identify any additional resources that you both agree are critical for accomplishing the task and offer to secure them.

5. Review the key points and check for understanding. Ask the other person to summarize the major points of agreement. If you are making a cross-functional assignment or assigning work to someone over whom you have no direct authority, be sure to explore the scope of the other person's commitments. Otherwise, conflicts in priorities may lead to a missed deadline. If you suspect a problem, ask the person directly whether he or she foresees any obstacles to carrying out the assignment. Offer help to remove them.

6. Agree on a date for an early progress review. Every task has its gray areas. Accordingly, you will need to set up checkpoints to review progress. If the person carrying out the task is new to the job or does not report directly to you, consider scheduling more checkpoints than you might otherwise. This allows you to deal with problems in time. Encourage the person to report how he or she is managing the task and to ask for coaching when needed.

Influencing for Win-Win Outcomes

Use this tool when you need to present a new idea, offer a solution, or make a strong case for change. Winning support for your ideas depends on communicating your ideas effectively, clearly establishing the benefits to others, and gaining the cooperation that leads to a specific plan for action.

Step 1. Plan the best approach.

Decide what you want to accomplish. When you're planning to influence someone, it's best to begin with the end in mind. What form of support are you looking for? It might help to visualize the end result you want and what it will take to achieve that result.

Identify the stakeholders and their needs. When you know what you want to accomplish, ask yourself these questions:

- Whose help will you need to accomplish your desired outcome?

- Whom will your proposal affect?
- Who might significantly interfere with implementing your proposal?

Once you've determined whose support you need, focus on one person at a time. Think about what motivates each person so you can match your proposal to individual needs. In particular, identify the factors you think would motivate a particular person to support your recommendation. Keep in mind the need to address factors that appeal to both reason and emotion. Consider the following list as a starting point:

- Saving time
- Applying logic, data, or information
- Using power or authority
- Gaining a sense of belonging
- Feeling needed
- Working for the greater good
- Having an opportunity to innovate
- Ensuring security and comfort
- Acting on practical considerations
- Gaining recognition
- Satisfying ambition
- Realizing achievement
- Being able to develop new abilities
- Increasing personal competence
- Getting control over outcomes
- Having a chance to be creative
- Pleasing others
- Improving workflow
- Reducing stress
- Increasing sales
- Making or saving money
- Reducing errors

Decide what benefits to stress based on the person you need to influence. A good idea will have benefits in many areas. But a well-targeted presentation will stress the benefits that motivate one particular person at a time.

Think about objections the person might have to your proposal. By thinking in advance about the objections, concerns, or obstacles the person might raise, you'll be better able to address them in a positive way.

Step 2. Establish mutual involvement in the situation.

Determine the best way to approach the person. In making your proposal, you want to meet a person on his or her own ground. How would he or she want to be approached (e.g., face-to-face, by phone, or in an e-mail message)?

Briefly describe the situation and how it affects both of you. Be as specific as possible about the effects of the problem. Describe how it makes work for both of you more difficult, more stressful, more costly, less satisfying, more time-consuming, or lower in quality or output.

> *The number of shipping errors has increased dramatically in the last six months. I know you get a lot of complaints about those errors in customer service, and they're causing us a lot of rework.*

Discuss the stake you both have in improving the situation.

> *Finding a way to reduce the number of errors would take a lot of pressure off the customer service reps—and it would save all of us a lot of time.*

Step 3. Explain your recommendation and its benefits.

Briefly explain your recommendation.

> *I'd like you to become part of a problem-solving team that's focused on getting at the root cause of these problems.*

Explain how the recommendation benefits the other person.

> *By participating on this team, you can make sure any plan the team develops addresses the interests of cus-*

tomer service. Plus, you'll be able to let the customer service reps know that help is on the way.

Explain how the recommendation benefits the organization.

Having input from customer service will speed up the process and help us find a solution that meets customer needs.

Explain how the recommendation benefits you.

Shipping can't solve this problem without help from other areas. We've been trying to do it alone, and we're not making the progress we need to.

Explain how your proposal will deliver the benefits. Benefits motivate people, but they need to link directly to your proposal.

Nobody else on the team has experience handling customer complaints.

Your input could help us target the biggest problems right away.

Step 4. Ask for reactions and address concerns.

Make sure the person understands your proposal. Ask questions to check for the person's full understanding of your main points.

What parts of my recommendation concern you or are unclear?

What questions do you have?

Use open-ended questions to ask for reactions to your idea or proposal. Ask for the person's opinion of your proposal.

What do you think of this idea?

Probe for negative reactions to get them out where you can deal with them.

Tell me about your concerns. What obstacles do you foresee?

Don't jump to conclusions about what someone means. Ask for an explanation. Be sure you understand the person's point of view before you address it.

Meet each negative reaction with a positive attitude of mutual problem solving. Restate each concern as you understand it. Clarify your proposal if you think a misunderstanding is the source of the concern, or offer any additional information that might alleviate the concern.

Ask for suggestions on how to address the concern before offering suggestions of your own. If it appears the person hasn't recognized the benefits you stated in Step 3, probe to come up with alternative benefits.

What would make this proposal work for you?

Step 5. Ask for the specific support you need and explain what you will do in return.

Ask for the specific support you need to implement your idea. Be very specific about what you need (e.g., time, money, approvals, people, or certain project parameters).

I need you to call five clients. Each call will take about an hour.

Explain what you will do in return. People are more likely to give support willingly if they see your own willingness to pitch in. If you're asking the person to take on more work, offer to take on some of it yourself.

I'll do the legwork for this. I'll call the clients in advance and send them the background materials. Afterwards, I'll have your notes transcribed for you.

If you're asking for other resources, explain which of your own resources you'll put toward your proposal.

I'm devoting 15 percent of my quarterly budget to this proposal. Your additional funds can make it happen.

Alternatively, you might be able to do something to make your idea more valuable from the other person's point of view.

I'll make sure you get copies of everyone's summaries so you'll have that information for your marketing plan.

Seal your agreement by reviewing the agreed-upon actions. Establish an action plan with clear roles and responsibilities. Set follow-up dates.

So we'll meet Tuesday morning to go over the latest product information.

Will you let me know then when you plan to review sales tools and training?

Express your appreciation for whatever level of commitment you have received so far, even if it isn't all you had hoped for.

Thank you for agreeing to help me with these calls. With your help, we'll be able to release the report before the deadline.

14

The "Team Formation Checklist"

This tool helps you and other team members gather critical information about the team and your role within it. This tool is useful in a number of situations. Use the checklist when a team:

- Is starting a new project
- Needs to adjust to a change in direction or plans
- Has difficulty meeting deadlines
- Has a new leader
- Is clarifying roles and responsibilities
- Is changing its focus or developing new goals

Step 1. Determine the change or problem affecting your team.

When a new team forms, the team leader or a senior manager usually gives team members essential background information, including why the team was created and how its mission fits into the organization's mission and goals. As you listen to the leader or manager present this information, record it. Ask questions to be sure you have all the information you need.

When the team changes direction, the Checklist will help you understand the scope of the change and the impact it will have on the team and on the team's purpose or mission. When you join an existing team, you may want to meet with one or more team members and ask them the Checklist questions.

Step 2. Complete the checklist with this change or problem in mind.

For each item, decide whether you have enough information for a full response; then check the appropriate box.

Team Formation Checklist

Yes	No	
☐	☐	1. What is the team's mission or purpose?
☐	☐	2. How does that mission fit into the larger organization's mission?
☐	☐	3. What are the expectations for this team? What specifically are we to accomplish?
☐	☐	4. What specific goals or milestones already exist?
☐	☐	5. If goals or milestones don't already exist, what is the time frame for developing them?
☐	☐	6. What is the time frame for results?
☐	☐	7. How will we get the information we need?
☐	☐	8. What resources will be available to us?
☐	☐	9. Will we be doing activities that we don't currently know how to do? If so, how will we get the training we need?
☐	☐	10. What process will we use to connect with the larger organization?
☐	☐	11. What time commitment will participation on this team require from each of us?
☐	☐	12. What is each team member's specific role? Long-term responsibilities?
☐	☐	13. What are the limits on our authority to make decisions?
☐	☐	14. Who approves decisions that are outside our limits?
☐	☐	15. What is our budget?
☐	☐	16. When will this team disband?

Step 3. Collect the missing information you need.

For items you have checked "no," ask the team leader, a senior manager, or others for the information you need to answer completely.

Step 4. Use this information to help your team create an action plan.

This Checklist will help each team member understand the scope of the team's assignment. Individual roles can become more targeted to the desired results.

Raising Difficult Issues with Your Team

This tool gives you some specific actions for communicating honestly about difficult or sensitive team issues. Use this tool to help you and other team members raise issues, define their scope, and gain the commitment you need before moving on to solve the problem. This tool is especially appropriate when you encounter issues like:

- Missed deadlines
- Difficulty in sharing resources
- Violation of team agreements
- Failure to meet performance expectations
- Technical differences of opinion
- Members functioning as individuals rather than team players
- Poor planning

Step 1. Request time to bring up an issue that may affect the team's performance.

Name the subject or topic you think the team needs to discuss.

I think we need to straighten out some training issues before we go any further.

For complex issues, especially ones that are not urgent, it is a good idea to ask for time at the next team meeting or to call a special meeting.

I know our agenda for the next meeting is full, but I would like 20 minutes to discuss our planning process for this task.

We aren't scheduled to meet as a team for another week, but I think we need a special meeting to discuss this planning issue.

For matters that won't wait, request time on the spot.

Could we shift gears for a minute to talk about an issue that affects what we'll all be doing during the next 24 hours?

If other team members ask for an explanation, give a brief one.

I am concerned that we are trying to accomplish this task without developing a plan.

I'm afraid that if we don't deal with this issue right now, we are going to have problems very soon.

Step 2. Describe what you have observed.

State your observations briefly and specifically. Describe a specific event or action, tell when and where it happened, and say who was involved.

We used different sets of questions when we called customers last week to get their input on the new ordering process. We didn't all use the set of questions we had agreed on.

Focus on the situation, issue, or behavior, not on the person.

I've noticed a pattern. When it comes to getting customer feedback, our process is inconsistent.

Don't give a solution to the situation.

I don't have a solution for this problem. All I'm trying to do is bring the situation to everyone's attention.

Step 3. Explain what you see as the possible impact on the team.

Describe the effects of the situation on the team (e.g., missed deadlines, errors, difficulties in accomplishing a task, need for rework, team credibility).

Because we asked customers different questions from those we agreed on, we are going to have a difficult time pulling our data together into a clear and simple format.

Quantify the impact (e.g., cost, time, quality).

The variety of questions we asked will mean that we'll have to spend more time analyzing the data we got. I'm estimating at least an additional week.

I'm concerned about the quality of information we gathered. This data will be used to fine-tune our ordering system over the next six months.

Describe the situation from different points of view (i.e., how customers, suppliers, other teams, or other team members see the issue).

From Shipping's point of view, the better our data, the better the service.

Step 4. Ask other team members to react to what you have said.

State the kind of participation you want.

How about each of you taking a minute to summarize how you see the situation?

Listen carefully. Don't plan your response while someone else is evaluating the situation, but don't be afraid to ask questions either. Give people time to organize their thoughts. Encourage others to speak up by indicating that you are receptive to their points of view.

Are you referring to the customer survey we conducted last month? I know what you mean. Those results caught most of us by surprise.

Avoid moving into a problem-solving mode. Remember to ask for reactions to what you've said rather than to ask the team how to solve the problem.

Without jumping into a solution, who has a comment about this situation?

Find ways to help other team members maintain their self-esteem. Sensitive subjects can lead to some heated discussions. It's important to listen to other team members in a nondefensive manner.

I know what you mean. Sometimes customers don't want to answer the questions; they'd rather talk about what's on their minds.

Include everyone in the discussion. You may need to draw out team members who are uncomfortable speaking in front of the whole group. The best way to do this is with a short question and by using the person's name.

Carl, you have been silent on this issue. How do you see the situation?

Be willing to move on if others don't think the issue needs addressing. Bringing up an issue with the team involves a series of small judgment calls. Knowing when you have done your part and when it's a good idea to move on comes with practice.

From everything we've said, this apparently is not something we have to deal with right now. It sounds as if we have the situation under control.

Step 5. Clarify and summarize what you have heard.

Your ability to clarify and summarize depends entirely on how well you listen to what each team member has to say. It might be difficult to remember everything everyone has said, so it's a good idea to invite each person to add or clarify as you summarize his or her feedback.

Paraphrase what you have heard. Accurately rephrasing what another person has said builds trust. It's also the surest way to check whether what you heard is what the person actually said. If I heard you correctly, Anne, you feel that the questions we agreed on meet our needs, and that to add or change our approach at this point would just complicate the task. Is that right?

> *Stan, your point is that after talking to a few customers, you realized that our questions miss some real customer concerns.*

If necessary, ask additional questions and paraphrase the responses.

> *I'm not sure I understand your point, Betsy. Would you give us an example of what you mean?*

After clarifying everyone's input, summarize the key points of the discussion. It isn't necessary to repeat everything everyone said. Focus on comments about what's getting in the team's way. Keep your summary objective; that is, don't try to evaluate.

> *So we agree on some consistent methods to use when surveying customers. What we don't agree on is how to handle unsolicited feedback.*

Step 6. Ask others to suggest the next steps.

Ask an open-ended question.

> *What shall we do about this situation?*
>
> *Now that we've agreed we have a problem, what should our next move be?*

If other team members do not suggest next steps, get the discussion going by proposing your own.

Here's an idea. What if we go back to our original survey questions and each fill in the information we got that relates to those questions? What do you all think?

Don't press for an on-the-spot solution to the situation or problem.

We can't solve the problem right here. The best we can do is figure out what we should do next.

Gain agreement from all team members on the next steps.

What do you think about the idea of seeing how many answers we have to the original survey questions? Does everyone think that makes sense?

Expressing Yourself: Presenting Your Thoughts and Ideas

Anytime you need to make a presentation before a group, whether in a formal or informal setting, you can use the guidelines for "Expressing Yourself" to organize your thoughts in an effective way.

Step 1. Formulate your objective.

Think of listeners as customers. Instead of focusing on what you want to accomplish, think of your listeners' needs and formulate your objective from their point of view. Whenever possible, use action verbs.

My listeners will be able to explain the new features in ProExacta version 3.5.

Team members will understand why their budget proposal wasn't approved, and they'll know what modifications to make.

At least half of the audience members will ask to be put on our mailing list.

Plan in advance. Take time to nail down a clear, concise statement of your objective. The clearer you are about your objective, the easier it will be to structure your talk.

If possible, put your objective in writing; then modify it as needed. Writing your objective will help you both to formulate your thoughts about your ultimate goal and to provide direction as you develop your supporting points.

Think before you start to speak. Whether you're speaking off the cuff or planning a formal presentation weeks ahead, advance planning will pay off—even when you only have a few seconds. If there isn't time to outline all your points, at least take the time to focus on your listeners and what you want them to understand, think, or do as a result.

Step 2. Capture interest.

Explain why to listen. To capture your listeners' interest, you need to go beyond just getting their attention, and let them know why your message is important to them. A clever introduction may grab listeners' attention initially, but their thoughts will soon stray unless your introduction clearly relates to your topic and to them. After all, your purpose isn't merely to capture people's interest, but to hold it.

Highlight benefits. One of the easiest ways to capture interest is to tell people how they can benefit from listening to your message.

I have an idea that could save us five hours of work a week.

Refer to common problems or goals. Everyone is interested in solving problems, maintaining values, and meeting goals. Let your listeners know how your talk will help.

I know this is hard to discuss, but if we don't act on this feedback now, we'll lose one of our biggest accounts.

Unless everyone follows these regulations and documents the process, we could face a major lawsuit.

This new system will help salespeople get fast, reliable information—which will help all of us.

Step 3. State your central point.

Keep it simple. Your central point doesn't need to be elaborate. In fact, it will probably be more memorable if it's simple and straightforward.

> *I'd like to see us set up a 10-minute meeting at the beginning of each shift.*

Summarize information. If you're communicating complicated information, structuring your central point as part of an overview of the facts can be helpful. The overview gives your listeners a focal point when you get into the details.

> *Overall, the response to the survey was very positive—86 percent of our clients are pleased with our service.*

> *Overall, our breakage losses were up 5 percent this month, which cost the company about $7,000.*

Step 4. Offer supporting points.

Organize in logical categories. People remember information more easily when it's organized into a few distinct categories.

> *This client interview form may seem overwhelming, but basically the questions help you ask clients about three things: their organization, their role, and their use of our product.*

Make supporting points come alive. Your supporting points will have more impact if you illustrate them with relevant information that appeals to your listeners.

Try using any of the following:

- Personal experiences
- Analogies
- Expert opinions
- Examples
- Facts and statistics
- Anecdotes
- Quotations

Use clear transitions. Transitions help your listeners follow you from point to point. Some ways to make transitions include the following:

- Use bridge words. These are words that tell your listeners you are shifting gears: furthermore, in addition, however, therefore, consequently, and finally.

- Trigger a transition with repetition. This involves using the same word twice to link one topic to the next.

- Ask a leading question. This involves asking a question you will go on to answer.

Hint. If transitions are difficult for you, try this: Instead of asking yourself, "How can I make people see that these two ideas are connected?" ask yourself, "How are these two ideas connected?" Often, you'll find that you already have a natural transition in mind.

Additional hints: Choose an appropriate sequence. Order your supporting points clearly and logically so your listeners can follow them easily. Possible ways to order your supporting points are:

- Chronological order
- Cause and effect
- Most important to least important
- Biggest to smallest
- Least expensive to most expensive
- Simple to complex

Limit details to the essentials. Don't swamp people with numbers, names, and other details that aren't essential to your objective. The fewer details you provide, the more likely people will remember the details you do provide.

Use language that the listeners can easily understand. Your listeners may be from different areas of the organization, have different backgrounds, and possess different levels of experience. Avoid special terminology, technical words, and abbreviations or acronyms that may not be familiar to some listeners.

Step 5. Summarize and recommend action.

Provide a quick summary. Reinforce your message by giving a quick summary of what you've covered. Be clear and concise; relate your summary to your central point.

Be straightforward. If your objective is for listeners to take a specific action, you're most likely to get results if you're direct at the very end. Be assertive. People are more inclined to take action if they see that you're not afraid to say what you want.

I recommend that you buy this equipment. I guarantee it will pay for itself within a year.

Let's start cross-training right away, so we'll all be prepared by summer.

TOOL

17

Moving from Conflict to Collaboration

This tool will help you take a planned, constructive approach to conflict situations. This approach is especially useful when you need to:

- Face a problem or issue early on, before the situation has an impact on productivity or morale.
- Confront a more experienced or senior employee.
- Handle conflicts with people whose backgrounds, responsibilities, or approaches are significantly different from your own.
- Get past the emotion so you can concentrate on the issue that's creating the conflict and its resolution.

Step 1. Establish mutual involvement.

Briefly describe the problem. Behind every conflict lies a problem—and you need to begin by stating it. Be objective. Do not give your opinions. Provide enough information for the other person to understand the issues and to make an informed response.

Establish the other person's stake. Point out the potential benefits of addressing the conflict, as well as the potential consequences of letting it go unresolved. Tie in issues that are important to the other person.

> *If we can address this issue, customer satisfaction should increase—and your department will have a lot less rework.*

State your positive intentions. Establish a sense of partnership by expressing your desire for mutual gain and your concern for maintaining a good working relationship. Let the other person know that your objective is not to place blame, but rather to fully understand and resolve the issues.

> *It's important for our groups to work well together. That's why I'm eager to resolve our differences.*

Step 2. Seek to understand the other person's point of view.

Assume and admit that you don't have all the information. Each person approaches a conflict with only a partial understanding of the issues involved. Let the other person know you are aware of this and that you need his or her help to fill in the gaps. This will emphasize your openness to another point of view.

Ask questions to bring out critical issues. Ask questions that will help expand your understanding of the situation. Cast a wide net initially. Use open-ended questions to probe for the other person's views. Without forcing the issue, try to bring out his or her underlying needs, fears, desires, and interests.

> *How does your group experience the problem?*
>
> *How does it affect you when we change the specifications?*
>
> *Why do you think the swing shift had such a problem with last week's revisions?*

Listen until you completely understand. Don't interrupt. Use silence and pauses to promote sharing. Use both verbal and nonverbal techniques to encourage the other person to express as much as possible. *Do not cut this portion of the conversation short.* It usually takes time to get beyond the other person's stated position and into his or her underlying interests and needs.

Check your understanding. Restate or paraphrase what you have heard. Acknowledge the other person's views and concerns. Express empathy, if appropriate.

> *So you're concerned because you need a week of lead time—and you're generally given about half of that.*

Offer an apology when appropriate. Realize that the other person may have legitimate complaints about your actions. An apology can bridge the gap between people and create an environment conducive to problem solving. A word of caution: Do not offer an apology as a ploy; only apologize when you are truly sorry.

Step 3. Present your perspective of the problem and its impact.

Use what you've learned from doing Step 2. Successful probing of the other person's interests and needs often brings out new issues that can impact not only your point of view, but also how you choose to express it and what points you want to highlight.

> *From what you've said, it's clear that there's a lot more to this than I first thought. . . .*

Describe the problem from your perspective. In terms the other person can easily understand, briefly explain how you experience the problem. Define the *what, who, when,* and *where* as you see them. If you try to address *why* and *how* at this point, the discussion may become subjective and slip into the hazardous realm of opinion and speculation.

> *In the case of last week's spec changes, we had to act quickly. Sales support told us that the customer had*

requested the tighter tolerances in the following week's shipment of product.

DO	DON'T
Emphasize that you're presenting your perspective.	Hint.
Make observations.	Generalize.
Use specific facts.	
Be objective and nonjudgmental.	Make assumptions.
Identify your feelings, desires, and needs.	Place blame.
Use neutral language.	
Use "I" statements.	

Describe the impact of the problem. Explain how you see the situation affecting you, others, and the business—with particular emphasis on the business. Focusing on the business reduces the risk of the discussion degenerating into a simple clash of personalities or individual needs.

When we're unable to do these changeovers routinely, they jeopardize our relationship with the customer and result in tremendous increases in overtime expenses.

Step 4. Decide on an appropriate plan of action.

Agree on the issues addressed. Revisit common interests and common goals. Review the facts related to the problem causing the conflict, drawing upon what you've learned in Step 2. Look for areas of agreement. If there are multiple issues, begin with the easy ones. Build on small successes to create a sense of momentum.

So, we agree that we need to meet the customer's expectations—and that our current system doesn't do that.

If no agreement seems possible, end the discussion. If at this point you can't find any common ground for agreement, you might consider:

- Agreeing to disagree for the time being and looking for ways to work around the problem.

- Disengaging yourself politely from the discussion and considering other approaches you can explore.

Identify the next logical step. Depending upon the situation, the next step could be:

- Agreeing upon an obvious resolution.

- Gathering information.

- Brainstorming possible solutions, then identifying the best solution—possibly by combining options.

- Applying a formal or informal problem-solving process.

- Seeking an objective third party to mediate.

Share responsibility for implementing your plan. Both parties must take responsibility for executing your joint resolution. Lead the way by personally committing to a specific action. Then ask the other person to commit to a specific action.

Document agreed-upon actions, accountability, and follow-up times. Formalizing your plan in writing can eliminate future confusion. Include the name of the person or people responsible for each step, and schedule dates and times to jointly evaluate progress. A written record is especially important when solutions are long-term ones.

Step 5. Express your appreciation for the other person's efforts.

Thank the other person. Express your appreciation to the other person for taking the time to work through the conflict with you.

Provide feedback. When appropriate, share specific information about how the other person contributed to the conflict's successful resolution. Share suggestions for better ways of dealing with any future conflicts. In this way, you can turn the conflict into an opportunity for learning, as well as for personal and professional development.

Summarize what you have learned. Make sure you learn at least one new thing from each conflict situation. This may be an insight into yourself and your approach to conflict. It may be new information about the other person that will allow you to work together more effectively in the future. Or it may be a better understanding of the situation at hand. In any case, let the other person know how working together to manage the conflict has contributed to your knowledge.

Thanks for taking the time to work this through. I have a much better understanding of your point of view now. I think this will make it much easier for us to collaborate in the future.

Handling Emotions under Pressure

This tool offers seven steps you can use with others to help them work through emotional situations. The techniques are effective when used in step by step order, but also they can be used in varying orders or combinations as the situation requires. Each provides a guideline for helping people work through their emotions so they can refocus their energy on productive problem solving.

Step 1. Acknowledge the person's emotion and describe its impact.

Describe what you hear or see. Be specific and objective.

Jim, you walked out of that meeting very abruptly. You seemed angry.

Describe the impact of the emotion. State how the person's behavior is affecting another individual, you, or the others involved.

The discussion started to focus on what had upset you, and we didn't know whether to proceed with the meeting.

Maintain the person's self-esteem. Communicate your concern and respect for the other person's feelings. Avoid negative phrases or anything that casts the behavior in a derogatory light. Make the other person aware that you understand the importance of the situation.

I know how hard you've worked on this project. It must be terribly frustrating to lose funding now that you're so close to completion.

Step 2. Invite the person to share thoughts and feelings.

Ask the person directly for his or her observations and opinions. Use open-ended questions.

What happened to make you so angry?

How do you think this situation relates to the recent changes?

What do you think is causing the problem?

Let the person vent his or her feelings. A person may just need a chance to air grievances. Expressing pent-up emotions often dispels them, allowing someone to view the situation more calmly.

Remain calm. If the other person's ranting exceeds your tolerance level or seems directed at you, you'll have to work hard to keep your own emotions in check. But even if you feel uncomfortable or are under attack, don't allow yourself to become defensive or confrontational, because that will only escalate the emotional situation. Also, be careful of overidentifying with the other person's emotions. You can be supportive without jumping on the bandwagon.

Use silence. Sometimes saying nothing can help the other person regain composure. Accompanying your silence with appropriate nonverbal cues, such as leaning forward and maintaining eye contact, will show that you are listening.

Step 3. Determine whether continuing the discussion is appropriate.

Ask the person if he or she wants to continue the discussion. The other person may want a cooling-off period or time for reflection. Time spent considering the consequences of emotional behavior and calming down can clear the way for a constructive conversation at a later time.

Would it be better if we got together later instead of discussing the situation right now?

Determine whether you can continue. You may be the one who needs to take some additional time before continuing the discussion. You may have been caught off guard, or you may be having difficulty keeping your own emotions under control.

There's a lot more here than I realized. I'd like to think about what you've said overnight. Can we meet again tomorrow around two?

Determine whether you are capable of dealing with the situation. No one is equipped to deal with every incident of emotional behavior. Don't try to play amateur psychologist or give advice outside your own area of expertise. If necessary, offer your support and refer the person to the appropriate channels.

This sounds like a serious complaint that HR should hear about.

Step 4. Listen to understand.

Concentrate on understanding; be aware of your own filters. Don't let your perceptions and beliefs get in the way of understanding. If you have the urge to interrupt, take a deep breath and remind yourself to listen.

Listen for both facts and feelings. When emotions run high, facts and feelings become intertwined. You'll need to understand both before resolving the underlying issues.

Pay attention to nonverbal cues. The effective listener perceives far more than the speaker's words. A person's posture, body movements, and facial expressions can speak volumes about his or her feelings and energy level. These nonverbal cues can convey not only a person's emotional state, but also how the person is coping with the emotions.

Step 5. Probe to uncover underlying issues.

Ask open-ended questions. How you read someone else's emotions is an approximation at best, especially because people who are caught up in emotions often have trouble expressing feelings or getting to the issues. Asking open-ended questions can help you (and the other person) clarify feelings and uncover the important issues.

> *What problems has your group had in finalizing the brochure's content?*
>
> *How do you feel about adding the western region to your service area?*

Step 6. Communicate your understanding.

Summarize the person's point of view. Summarizing the other person's viewpoint communicates your desire to understand without indicating whether you agree. Focus on those areas with which the person is having the most difficulty. Ask if you have understood the message.

> *Am I correct that you don't feel the decision about when to launch the campaign was fair to your team?*

If the person says you don't understand, explain that you want to. Ask for examples. Make sure you take responsibility for not understanding. Placing blame on the other person by saying something like, "You don't make sense," will only escalate the situation or cause the person to withdraw.

> *I guess I don't realize the consequences well enough to understand. Can you give me an example of the kind of thing you're having to deal with?*

Remember that it's important to validate the person's feelings even if you disagree. You don't have to agree to understand.

> *It sounds as if Pat's comments really hurt you.*

Express your confidence in the other person's ability to deal effectively with the situation. Let the other person know that you believe in his or her abilities. This is not the time to criticize or make a value judgment. Remind the person of past successes or simply say that you value his or her contributions.

I'm sure you'll be able to straighten this out. After all, you were the one who worked out the misunderstanding over the retooling schedule.

Provide assurances (if appropriate). If appropriate, let the other person know that you will take the time necessary to address the issues. If the level of help required is beyond your scope, direct the person to someone who *can* help.

Step 7. Help the person move on.

Ask what can be done to resolve the underlying issues. Ask the person what solution, if any, he or she thinks would help. Your task is not to solve the problem but to help generate effective responses and/or provide a different perspective, especially if the person sees no solution.

This might look better from the sales end. Have you talked to a sales rep?

Acknowledge feelings, but help identify issues. Once a person trusts your intent, help that person accept his or her underlying feelings and isolate the work-related issues.

It's hard not to see this as a lot of extra work for nothing, but how might these new procedures tie into our implementation of the new technology?

Refocus on the work-related issues. Suggest ways to deal with the issues. Offer support or suggest other sources.

It might help to talk to Rich. He seems to understand the new system better than just about anyone except the techs.

Be flexible and open. Be willing to make some concessions to resolve the issues. You may have to modify your own plans to help the other person move forward.

I'd be happy to call Rich and set up a meeting, if you think that would help.

Cultivate a short memory. As soon as the emotional behavior is over, it's over. Don't dwell on it. Put the episode behind you and focus on the work.

Executive Leadership Study

Lilanthi Ravishankar and Kathleen Hurson

Purpose

The primary goal of this study was to determine the leadership qualities that top executives in North America consider critical to organizations. A previous study of human resources executives undertaken by AchieveGlobal indicated that, for organizational improvement strategies to take root, a cohesive vision was a critical leadership characteristic needed within organizations. The present study surveyed top management and their direct reports to determine executive perspectives on the leadership characteristics critical to successful organizations.

Method

Participants. The sample consisted of a total of 353 senior executives—143 top managers with the actual titles or functional equivalents of CEO, COO, president, or chairman, as well as 210 of their direct reports. Of these, 303 interviews were held with executives in the United States, while 50 were with Canadian executives. The interviewees represented a cross-section of industries, including finance, manufacturing, health care, retail, transportation/telecommunications/ energy, and the U.S. federal government. All corporate interviews were with executives in companies having at least 350 employees.

Materials. The survey contained 14 closed-ended items and 4 open-ended items. The response scale was a 4-point scale ranging from "not at all important" to "very important." Respondents were also given the option of choosing "not sure" as a response. A series of items explored the characteristics of leadership from the perspective of senior executives. One of the open-ended items asked executives what they felt were the most important characteristics of a leader. A closed-ended item provided executives with a list of leadership characteristics taken from the leadership literature and asked them to rate each characteristic's importance. Another item asked executives for their opinion on what critical leadership characteristics would be needed by future leaders.

Procedures. An external research firm was commissioned to conduct the telephone interviews with executives. Each interview lasted approximately 30 minutes.

Analyses. The data were tabulated using frequency and percentage distributions. The open-ended comments were categorized.

Results

The most frequent response to the unprompted, open-ended item regarding the most admirable characteristic of a leader was *integrity*. By far, the most frequent response included some aspect of integrity, such as *honesty, ethics,* or even *integrity* itself. Over one-third of CEOs and COOs (38%), as well as a similar proportion of their direct reports (36%), employed one of these three words when prompted for the most admirable leadership characteristics. This was true across the spectrum of industries surveyed.

Vision was named as another admired characteristic of leaders. Besides integrity, vision was the only attribute mentioned by over one-quarter of the executives as an admirable quality of leaders.

Following their open-ended, unprompted assessment of critical leadership characteristics, executives were asked to rate the importance of selected phrases describing leaders that were derived from a previous leadership study. These characteristics were *setting a vision, managing change, managing business processes, displaying technical skill, taking risks, putting customer needs first, possessing strong interpersonal skills, making credible presentations, being outspoken,* and *showing compassion.* Four of these characteristics were rated as "very important" by over three-quarters of the executives. These were *setting a vision* (rated "very important" by 93% of respondents), *managing change* (87%), *interpersonal skills* (85%), and *putting customer needs first* (80%).

Following their assessment of the qualities of current leaders, executives were asked to comment on what characteristics future leaders, in contrast to current leaders, would need. Executives cited *vision* (28%) and the *ability to manage change* (20%) as critical for future leaders. Executives also cited *technical/computer skills,* an attribute that was regarded as considerably more important for future than for current leaders (13% of executives said it was very important for future leaders versus 8% for current leaders). This attribute was the third most frequently mentioned important characteristic of future leaders.

Discussion

The findings from this study indicate that leaders across the organizational hierarchy are in agreement about what constitutes good leadership. In identifying characteristics important in a leader, executives in this study cited three of the five leadership characteristics that compose the CLIMB model of leadership, which is based on over 1,500 critical incidents gathered from leaders at all levels in organizations. The components of the CLIMB model are: Create a compelling future, Let the customer drive the organization, Involve every mind, Manage work horizontally, and Build personal credibility. The corresponding characteristics mentioned by executives are *vision* (which corresponds to "Create a compelling future" in the CLIMB model), *putting customer needs first* (which corresponds to "Let the customer drive the organization" in the CLIMB model), and *ethics* or *integrity* (which corresponds to "Build personal credibility" in the CLIMB model). Although *managing change* does not link back directly to one of the main CLIMB categories, it is interesting to note that managing change is one of the competencies subsumed under the "Create a compelling future" component of the CLIMB model of leadership.

Teams and Quality: A Blended Strategy Works Best

Darlene Russ-Eft, Lilanthi Ravishankar,
and Linda Moran

Purpose

The purpose of this study was to understand and evaluate the role of teams, quality, and process improvement in creating competitive advantage.

Method

Participants. Of the 4,500 surveys distributed to potential respondents across the United States, 78 were undeliverable. From the remaining potential sample of 4,422 respondents, 985 (22%) responded. The survey respondents were from the following functional areas:

Human resources professionals: 51%

Quality assurance: 24%

Other departments: 24%

Survey respondents were classified into the following positions:

Directors or managers: 61%

Vice presidents: 12%

Specialists: 10%

Supervisors: <4%

Other positions: 15%

Approximately 44% of the respondents were from service industries and 56% from product-related companies.

Materials.   A 25-item survey was developed to determine the factors associated with these elements:

- The adoption of TQM and team efforts.
- The success of TQM and team efforts.
- The management of strategic processes.

A mailing house was retained to mail out the survey and supporting materials. The supporting materials included a cover letter and a business reply envelope.

Procedures.   A pilot test of selected survey items was conducted on the telephone with AchieveGlobal clients before the mailing was undertaken. Following the administration of a mock survey, respondents underwent a debriefing to determine whether the survey items were clear and understandable. The survey was revised accordingly.

To improve the response rate, the survey materials were mailed out in two phases. The same sample of participants received both mailings.

A follow-up survey with a random sample of nonrespondents was carried out to determine if there were any systematic differences between respondents and nonrespondents. Although respondents and nonrespondents were basically similar, there were some systematic differences. Nonrespondents felt their organizations' quality and team efforts were more successful than did respondents. Accordingly, the survey responses regarding the overall success of these efforts underestimate the actual success of the efforts.

Analyses.   To investigate the relationship between responses and the characteristics of organizations and respondents, survey responses were cross-tabulated by type of industry, work site size, and respondent's department. Parametric (*t*-tests and multiple-comparison tests) and nonparametric tests (chi-squared and median tests) of statistical significance were used to determine if there were systematic differences in the response patterns of the various types of individuals and organizations.

Results

The results indicate that two-thirds (66%) of quality efforts are "progressing but still facing numerous challenges" and 10% "continuously exceed expectations." Team initiatives are nearly as successful, with nearly two-thirds (61%) "progressing but still facing numerous challenges" and 10% "continuously exceeding expectations."

The majority of respondents reported having a quality effort (74%) or team initiative (71%) in place in their organization. Their reasons for adopting a TQM or team initiative were generally similar:

- To improve the quality of products and services (for this purpose, 85% adopted TQM, and 79% adopted a team effort)
- To improve productivity (78% chose TQM, and 78% chose teams)

The reason given as most important for adopting TQM was to improve customer satisfaction (87%); the reason that was most important in adopting a team initiative was to improve participation (81%).

These initiatives yielded many benefits, including increased employee participation (67% of respondents reported this as a benefit from TQM, 72% from teams) and improvements in the quality of products and services (66% from TQM, 63% from teams). However, benefits for the most part failed to match expectations. Most of the organizations achieved many of the expected benefits, but few achieved all. For example, while 87% of the respondents indicated that they adopted TQM to improve customer satisfaction, fewer than two-thirds (65%) reported this as a benefit.

Factors associated with the successful implementation of a

program, whether a quality or team initiative, were connected to the buy-in by the organization as a whole and, in particular, by those in executive and managerial positions. Success was significantly associated with these conditions:

- Programs that were integrated into the business plan.

- Executives and managers who actively supported and believed in the importance of the effort.

- The absence of strong resistance and/or sabotage of the programs.

- A coordinated or integrated program in which both a quality and a team effort were active in the organization.

Almost three-fourths (74%) of the organizations are managing some or all strategic processes. As with the team and quality efforts, a willingness by the organization and especially by the top leaders is very important in the successful management of strategic processes. In fact, many organizations indicated that their executives had identified key strategic processes (63%) or were serving as executive owners of some strategic processes (63%).

Respondents had strong opinions on what advice they would offer their CEOs for making their organizations more competitive. Among the 29% of respondents who provided comments, the ideas mentioned most frequently were "give us direction," "relinquish control and empower people," "walk the talk," "invest in quality people—train," and "focus on the customer."

Discussion

The findings of this study indicate that integrated approaches to change initiatives are strongly associated with success. Sound leadership also emerges as an important element in the success of such initiatives. When respondents were asked for opinions on what could be done to increase competitiveness, the most common themes were that leaders needed to empower employees, model the behaviors they expected employees to exhibit, and provide a coherent vision for the organization. Furthermore, it is clear that leadership support is essential for any kind of change initiative to be successful.

APPENDIX

C

Validation of the Measurement of Leadership Competencies among Executives

Judith Richterman, Kathleen Hurson, and Darlene Russ-Eft

Purpose

The purpose of this series of studies was to determine whether a valid and reliable instrument based on the CLIMB model of leadership could be developed and used for measurement with members of executive teams, their direct reports, and others within the same organization. A second purpose was to determine whether the measurement intervention affected the executive teams and the organizations.

Method

Participants. The participants came from six different organizations: two medical centers, a paper mill, a distribution company, an insurance company, and an airline company. The participants included executives ($n = 51$), direct reports ($n = 195$), and others ($n = 358$), with roughly 3 or 4 direct reports and between 7 and 10 others for each executive respondent.

Materials.   Instruments were designed to use the CLIMB model in measuring the leadership competencies of executives. Separate instruments, each consisting of 55 items, were created: one for use by executives, one for their direct reports, and one for others in the organization. Each item required two ratings: "agreement" and "importance." The agreement rating measured how much respondents agreed with a given statement, and the importance rating measured how important that person felt the item was to the organization. Both scales used a 7-point Likert-type scale. The agreement scale ranged from 1 to 7, with 1 representing "strongly disagree" and 7 representing "strongly agree." The importance scale also ranged from 1 to 7, with 1 representing "not at all important" and 7 representing "very important."

Procedures.   Each executive was given a questionnaire to complete. In addition, he or she received questionnaires to distribute to direct reports and to others in the organization. The questionnaires were returned in separate self-addressed envelopes. Results from the three groups were presented to the executive team at each organization.

Analyses.   Cronbach alphas were calculated overall and for each rating scale and each group. A principal components factor analysis using all 55 items, followed by a varimax rotation, was undertaken with each rating scale and each reporting group separately. These same analyses were performed using items from each predetermined factor in the CLIMB model.

Results

The Cronbach alphas on both agreement and importance revealed a high degree of internal consistency on almost all items. All items within the factor "Let the customer drive the organization" obtained lower alphas than other items. These ranged from .68 to .72. All other items obtained alphas of .87 or higher. This means that the items provide a good representation of the domain.

Factor analysis results on the agreement ratings from each of the three reporting groups indicate that the factor structure of the instrument and the CLIMB model are congruent. The factor analyses of items from each predetermined factor revealed that each factor emerged as unitary.

The executive teams from all six organizations participated in their own feedback session. In all cases, the teams used the feedback to develop plans for improving individual or team behaviors and interactions.

Discussion

One conclusion from this study is that an instrument assessing each of the factors underlying the CLIMB model of leadership can be developed and that these factors are independent. In addition, executives feel that information provided by such an instrument, presented in the context of this model, is useful for developing individual and team improvement plans. Furthermore, some organizations have used this intervention as a way to monitor changes over time.

Study to Define Leadership Competencies

Darlene Russ-Eft, Caryl Berrey, and Kathleen Hurson

Purpose

This study gathered critical incidents from individuals at all levels within a wide spectrum of organizations. The purpose was to develop a model of leadership among those in formal leadership positions as well as those not holding formal leadership positions. Part of the purpose of this study was to determine whether the competencies of those not holding formal leadership positions were the same or different from those in formal leadership positions.

Method

Participants. Respondents came from a variety of organizations, including heavy manufacturing, high-tech manufacturing, financial services, health and social services, business services, retail and distribution, transportation and utilities, government, and education. The study included organizations ranging in size from fewer than 250 employees to more than 10,000 employees from all of the major regions of the United States and Canada. These organizations had one thing in common: all had seen above-average growth in the number of employees over the past three years.

Interviewers contacted 915 organizations and completed interviews at 469 organizations (a response rate slightly higher than 50%). One or two managers or one or two nonmanagers were interviewed at each of the cooperating organizations. The total sample size was 761; about half of the sample were managers and half nonmanagers.

Materials.   The interviewers asked two main critical-incident questions:

1. Think of a time in the past month when a person in your organization showed good leadership.

    What did the person do that showed good leadership?

    What was the result of this behavior?

    What was the person's position in your organization?

2. Think of a time in the past month when a person in your organization showed poor leadership.

    What did the person do that showed poor leadership?

    What was the result of this behavior?

    What was the person's position in your organization?

In addition to the questions on leadership, interviewers asked questions regarding the characteristics of the respondent, such as job title.

Analyses.   The responses to each question were entered into a database along with information identifying the characteristics of the participants. Each incident identified as "critical" by the respondent, or judged by the analyst as so intended, was considered as a separate event. In some of these events, the subject of the incident did several things that showed either good or poor leadership. Because the unit of analysis in critical-incident studies is the specific behavior, duplicates of the entire response were entered so that each specific instance of good or poor leadership behavior could be analyzed as a separate entity. This procedure permitted the analyst to review the different incidents for classification purposes, while still being able to identify the entire response.

A total of 1,871 usable critical incidents were obtained from the sample. Of these incidents, 1,264 described the actions of a manager or supervisor and 607 described the actions of a nonsupervisor. The only responses not used in the analysis were those that were clearly not an incident or were uninterpretable.

The analysis of the incidents followed the guidelines set forth by Flanagan (1954) and Russ-Eft (1995) The steps included the following:

1. Select a general frame of reference.

2. Sort a sample of incidents into a limited number of piles in accordance with the frame of reference selected.

3. Formulate tentative headings for major areas.

4. Sort additional incidents into these major areas and set up new subcategories as necessary. During this process, all incidents considered so similar that they would remain together regardless of changes in category definitions were clipped together and treated as a unit.

5. Prepare tentative definitions for major headings as well as generalized statements for each of the main categories of incidents.

6. Make a tentative selection of the level of specificity/generality to be used in reporting the definition.

7. Redefine major areas and categories as necessary while incidents were being classified.

8. Review definitions and revise where necessary after all incidents had been classified.

9. Record the classification of each incident.

10. Have an independent check made of the classification of all incidents.

Competencies can be thought of as embedded components of a molecular structure of human behavior. In such a model, the behavioral indicators called critical incidents comprise the "subatomic particles." These critical incidents can be classified into larger units called competencies, or atoms. Such competencies can be classified into larger sets of competencies, or elements. Finally, a set of competencies can be classified into even larger sets, or molecules.

Thus, a number of critical incidents (called behavioral indicators or subatomic particles), such as "Got the staff connected to PC systems without being given step by step directions," and "Single-handedly started recycling projects throughout the company," were grouped into a competency labeled "Takes initiative to solve a problem." These, in turn, were placed, along with other lower-level competencies (such as "Implements good ideas," "Works extra hours or unsupervised," and "Helps others") under a broader competency, such as "Taking responsibility."

The critical-incident methodology did not involve a statistical analysis of a representative sample. The purpose was not to identify the most frequently mentioned leadership attributes, but rather to uncover the full range of critical attributes that make up leadership, regardless of organizational level.

Results

The major findings can be found in Table D.1. They were:

1. Leadership can be defined in terms of 17 competencies.

2. These 17 leadership competencies describe leadership at all levels of management, from the CEO to the frontline supervisor. They are also found among nonsupervisory employees.

3. These competencies align with earlier research, described in Appendix C, on successful executive behaviors.

Discussion

The most important conclusion indicated by the results of the critical-incident study was that leadership behaviors are practiced by both supervisory and nonsupervisory employees. There are, however, differences among the five CLIMB strategies. "Create a compelling future" shows the lowest number of

Table D.1 Listing of Competencies by Employment Level (Using the CLIMB Strategies)

CLIMB Strategy and Competency	Non-supervisory	Supervisory	Total	Total, as the Percentage (%), of the Grand Total

Create a compelling future
  Setting or sharing a vision
  Managing a change
	18	111	129	7%

Let the customer drive the
  organization
  Focusing on the customer
	32	34	66	3%

Involve every mind
  Dealing with individuals
  Supporting teams and
    groups
  Sharing information
  Solving problems, making
    decisions
	190	738	928	50%

Manage work horizontally
  Managing business
    processes
  Managing projects
  Displaying technical skills
  Managing time and
    resources
	159	152	311	17%

Build personal credibility
  Taking responsibility
  Taking initiative beyond
    job requirements
  Handling emotions
  Displaying professional
    ethics
  Showing compassion
  Making credible
    presentations
	208	229	437	23%

Grand total			1,871	100%

incidents involving nonsupervisory employees. In contrast, "Let the customer drive the organization" showed about the same number of incidents for supervisory and nonsupervisory personnel. "Involve every mind" contained the largest number of incidents, and most of these focused on those in supervisory positions. Finally, "Manage work horizontally" and "Build personal credibility" showed about the same number of incidents for supervisors and nonsupervisors.

Validation of Leadership Competencies among Individual Contributors

Darlene Russ-Eft and Caryl Berrey

Purpose

The purpose of this study was to determine whether a valid and reliable instrument based on the CLIMB model of leadership could be developed and used for measurement with individual contributors.

Method

Participants. A total of 129 people participated in the study. They came from 10 different organizations representing manufacturing, food processing, financial services, business services, educational services, and health services. All held nonsupervisory (professional or technical) positions.

Materials. The instrument was designed to measure the leadership competencies of nonsupervisory, professional/technical employees using the CLIMB model. It included 36 items. Each item was scored using a 5-point Likert-type scale.

The scale ranged from 1 to 5, with 1 representing "strongly disagree" and 5 representing "strongly agree."

Procedures. A contact person within each organization was selected to distribute questionnaires. Each subject received a questionnaire and a self-addressed stamped envelope for returning the questionnaire.

Analyses. A principal components factor analysis using all 36 items, followed by a varimax rotation, was undertaken. These same analyses were performed using items from each predetermined factor of the CLIMB model.

Results

The overall alphas and the item alphas revealed a high level of internal consistency. The overall alpha was .89, and the item alphas ranged from .88 to .89.

Results of the factor analyses on the agreement ratings indicated that the factor structures of the instrument and of the CLIMB model are congruent. The factor analyses of items from each predetermined factor revealed that each factor emerged as unitary.

Discussion

The critical-incident study described in Appendix D and the study of executive teams described in Appendix C, together with these results, provide further evidence for the construct validity of the CLIMB model of leadership. In addition, such validation extends to those holding leadership positions in organizations as well as to those who are not currently in such formal leadership positions. Given the trend toward flatter organizational structures, these results provide further evidence of the exercise of leadership at all levels in organizations.

Leadership Training at All Levels

Lilanthi Ravishankar and Julie Winkle

Purpose

The purpose of the study was to evaluate the effectiveness of a leadership training program designed to help individuals at all organizational levels acquire leadership behaviors. The specific program was *Leadership2000,* developed by AchieveGlobal. A critical-incident study had previously defined the key leadership competencies that formed the basis of the training program.

Method

The construction of a framework for this study adhered loosely to the Kirkpatrick typology of the four levels of evaluation: reaction (level 1), learning (level 2), skill transfer (level 3), and return on investment (level 4) (Kirkpatrick, 1959a,b; 1960a,b; 1995). The main deviation from the Kirkpatrick typology is that the results of the evaluation were intended to be used in a formative manner—that is, to modify the content of the leadership program as well as the instruments.

Participants.   The sample consisted of trainees and their managers from six organizations that participated in a pilot test of the leadership program. Included were banking, manufacturing, health care, and education. Trainees included supervisory and nonsupervisory employees. A total of 105 trainees completed mastery tests before training, and 67 after training. To gather data regarding the transfer of training to the workplace (level 3 data), a total of 81 training participants and 72 managers from the six organizations were surveyed at the start of training and approximately one month after the training was completed. Finally, level 4 data was gathered by conducting in-depth telephone interviews with a sample consisting of a subset of 16 trainees and 12 of their managers who completed level 3 surveys. To obtain an additional perspective, the interviews also included three training administrators.

Materials.   Mastery tests were administered to trainees before and after the training to assess trainees' knowledge and awareness of the concepts covered in training (level 2 data). The test items were presented in a variety of formats, including multiple choice, true/false, and requests for critical incidents (i.e., information about specific events demonstrating how leadership training was incorporated into leadership behaviors). A scoring key was devised for scoring the items, with critical incidents scored by awarding points on the extent to which trainees, in their workplace interactions, used the skills taught in the leadership training.

Because the training program was modular and each organization implemented different modules, customized questionnaires were created for each organization. The survey items used a 7-point Likert-type scale, with 1 representing "not at all" and 7 representing "to a very great extent," to measure the extent to which a particular behavior was used/observed on the job.

The posttraining survey (level 3) was designed to measure both how trainees applied their skills after the training (e.g., "To what extent do you confront a situation with a potential for conflict early on?") and, in retrospect, how they had applied the skills before training (e.g., "To what extent *did* you confront situations with a potential for conflict early on?"). By adjusting for greater awareness about the skills covered in training, this method provides an additional measure of the trainees' skill improvements.

Procedures. Mastery tests (level 2), as well as surveys measuring skills, were administered at the first training session and again approximately one month after the training. In addition, telephone interviews conducted with trainees and their managers after the training gathered critical incidents of how these skills were used, as well as descriptions of the impact that using such a skill had on both the work group and, ultimately, the organization. Because some research studies have shown that individual reaction to the training has little bearing on skill acquisition or transfer (Bretz and Thompsett, 1992; Dixon, 1990), no formal feedback was gathered on participants' reactions to the training (level 1). However, as a corollary to data gathered relative to level 4 results, information was obtained on participants' reactions to the training they received.

Because different combinations of the training modules were used by the different organizations, the data was tabulated by organization.

Analyses. Some basic analyses conducted on the data included means and standard deviations pre- and posttraining for level 2 and level 3 data. Although *t*-tests were conducted on the data from one organization that had a slightly larger sample relative to the others, no significant differences were found between pre- and posttraining scores, even though the actual

Table F.1   Pre- and Posttraining Knowledge Gains (Grand Means)*

	Pre	Post	Difference
Company 3	1.11	2.18	1.07
Company 4	1.11	2.08	0.97
Company 5	1.09	2.06	0.97
Company 2	1.90	2.53	0.63
Company 1	1.03	1.10	0.07

*Note that trainees from one of the organizations (Company 6) did not complete mastery (level 2) surveys.

differences in the ratings were discernible (see Table F.1). This is very likely an artifact of sample size. Due to the small size of the samples from the other organizations, the decision was to gather more data before conducting further analyses. In addition, some qualitative analyses of anecdotal level 4 type data were conducted.

Results

Results of the data analyses indicate the following for each level of data:

- **Trainees' reactions to the training (level 1 results).** Telephone interviews with trainees and their managers indicated that the training was well received by trainees. Both groups felt that the skills learned in training would be useful to them in their work.

- **Knowledge gains (level 2 results).** In general, trainees showed an overall improvement in their knowledge and awareness of the skills covered in the training (see Table F.1).

- **Skill transfer (level 3 results).** Trainees and their managers saw improvements in trainees' skills reflected in both pre- and posttraining evaluations and in the retrospective assessment of training effectiveness (see Tables F.2 and F.3). Both groups indicated that trainees were practicing many of the skills acquired in training to a greater extent than before the training. These ratings were relatively consistent across the various organizations, indicating that the questionnaires had face validity.

- **Bottom-line impact on the work group and the organization (level 4 results).** In-depth interviews indicated that trainees and their managers had a clear view of how skill improvements were tied to the organization's bottom line. The following examples of anecdotal data indicate that managers and trainees see a bottom-line impact on the organization as the result of increased use of the skills on the job.
  Managers. ". . . [A]n outcome is that when people

Table F.2 Pre- and Posttraining Skill Transfer (Grand Means) for Self-Ratings

	Pretraining	Posttraining	Difference
Company 1			
Managing your priorities	4.26	4.98	0.72
Moving from conflict to collaboration	4.53	5.14	0.61
Personal strategies for navigating change	5.08	5.63	0.55
Handling emotions under pressure	4.71	5.22	0.51
Giving and receiving constructive feedback	4.73	5.19	0.46
Company 2			
Managing your priorities	4.27	5.31	1.04
Proactive listening	5.10	5.97	0.87
Giving and receiving constructive feedback	4.71	5.55	0.84
Company 3			
Handling emotions under pressure	4.97	5.47	0.50
Moving from conflict to collaboration	5.09	5.58	0.49
Giving and receiving constructive feedback	5.04	5.46	0.42
Company 4			
Moving from conflict to collaboration	4.21	5.71	1.50
Influencing for win-win outcomes	4.09	5.56	1.47
Managing your priorities	3.99	5.38	1.39
Company 5			
Basic principles	4.83	5.97	1.14
Influencing for win-win outcomes	4.70	5.84	1.14
Managing your priorities	5.19	6.05	0.86
The leader in each of us	5.43	6.13	0.70
Company 6			
Influencing for win-win outcomes	4.09	5.74	1.65
Moving from conflict to collaboration	4.01	5.56	1.55
Basic principles	4.24	5.69	1.45

Table F.3 Pre- and Posttraining Skill Transfer (Grand Means) as Rated by Managers

	Pretraining	Posttraining	Difference
Company 1			
Managing your priorities	4.64	5.50	0.86
Giving and receiving constructive feedback	5.28	5.57	0.29
Handling emotions under pressure	5.42	5.54	0.12
Moving from conflict to collaboration	5.33	5.42	0.09
Personal strategies for navigating change	5.42	5.50	0.08
Company 2			
Managing your priorities	4.44	5.09	0.65
Company 3			
Handling emotions under pressure	3.72	4.44	0.71
Moving from conflict to collaboration	3.84	4.16	0.32
Giving and receiving constructive feedback	4.02	4.14	0.12
Company 4			
Influencing for win-win outcomes	4.23	5.43	1.20
Moving from conflict to collaboration	4.34	5.36	1.02
Managing your priorities	3.95	4.70	0.75
Company 5			
Basic principles	4.17	5.67	1.50
Influencing for win-win outcomes	4.27	5.73	1.46
Managing your priorities	4.72	5.71	0.99
The leader in each of us	5.10	5.80	0.70
Company 6			
Influencing for win-win outcomes	5.34	6.16	0.82
Moving from conflict to collaboration	5.30	6.08	0.78
Basic principles	5.52	6.20	0.68

call, it doesn't become a bigger problem; it doesn't get exacerbated or extended. She generally brings closure to most issues. The benefit to the district is that it saves a lot of people a lot of time."

". . . better production, less company loss monetarily, because when accounts are worked properly, we save money. I have seen where it has enabled us to work out a plan with a customer instead of foreclosing. . . . [Y]ou can see a decrease in the delinquency and a smaller inventory in foreclosure properties. That's hard-core evidence right there in black and white. . . ."

Trainees. ". . . I have a whole file of concerns that have been resolved. We have 25 schools in this area, and we don't have any unresolved concerns at this point."

". . . You cut out the complaints and all that. . . . We just, in the past two audits that we've had, have been excellent, whereas before they were marginal. You could just see the difference. Coming from marginal to excellent—that's a big accomplishment."

In addition to these anecdotes, these organizations also indicated that they would be able to provide hard data such as phone logs and transcripts to substantiate skill improvements.

Discussion

The results of the evaluation of the leadership program indicate that trainees were able to transfer their learning to the job successfully. The study indicates that individuals at different levels in organizations were able to acquire and demonstrate these skills. Critical-incident data also indicate that such skills do have a positive impact on participants' productivity and efficiency and, by extrapolation, on the organization's bottom line.

NOTES

CHAPTER 1

1. This discussion is loosely based on concepts in *Upsizing the Individual in the Downsized Organization: Managing in the Wake of Reengineering, Globalization, and Overwhelming Technology Change* by Robert Johnsen and Rob Swigart (Reading, MA: Addison-Wesley Publishing Company, 1996, pp. 15–20).

2. George T. Silvestri, "Occupational employment projections to 2006," *Monthly Labor Review,* 120 (November 1997): pp. 58–83.

3. See the Appendix for a more complete discussion of this study and other related AchieveGlobal research.

CHAPTER 3

1. Blake E. Ashforth and Ronald H. Humphrey, "Emotional Labor in Service Roles: The Influence of Identity," *Academy of Management Review* (January 1993). We are grateful to the authors for this discussion of emotional labor.

BIBLIOGRAPHY

CREATE A COMPELLING FUTURE (CHAPTER 2)

Brill, P. L., and R. Worth. *The Four Levers of Corporate Change.* New York: American Management Association, 1997.

Connor, D. R. *Managing at the Speed of Change: How Resilient Managers Succeed and Prosper Where Others Fail.* New York: Villard Books, 1992.

Heifetz, D. Laurie. "The Work of Leadership." *Harvard Business Review* (January–February 1997): 124–134.

Jacobs, R. W. *Real-Time Strategic Change: How to Involve an Entire Organization in Fast and Far-Reaching Change.* San Francisco: Berrett-Koehler Publishers, 1994.

Jellison, J. M. *Overcoming Resistance: A Practical Guide to Producing Change in the Workplace.* New York: Simon & Schuster, 1993.

Kotter, J. "Leading Change: Why Transformation Efforts Fail." *Harvard Business Review* (March–April 1995): 59–67.

Larkin, T. J., and S. Larkin. *Communicating Change: Winning Support for New Business Goals.* New York: McGraw-Hill, 1994.

Nadler, D. A., et al. *Discontinuous Change: Leading Organizational Transformation.* San Francisco: Jossey-Bass, 1995.

O'Toole, J. *Leading Change: Overcoming the Ideology of Comfort and the Tyranny of Custom.* San Francisco: Jossey-Bass, 1995.

Price Waterhouse Change Integration Team, The. *Better Change: Best Practices for Transforming Your Organization.* Burr Ridge, IL: Irwin, 1995.

Robinson, A. G., and S. Stern. *Corporate Creativity: How Innovation and Improvement Actually Happen.* San Francisco: Berrett-Koehler, 1997.

Shank, R. *Tell Me a Story.* Evanston, IL: Northwestern University Press, 1990.

Strebel, P. "Why Do Employees Resist Change?" *Harvard Business Review* (May–June 1996): 86–92.

Weisbord, M. R., and S. Janoff. *Future Search: An Action Guide to Finding Common Ground in Organizations and Communities.* San Francisco: Berrett-Koehler, 1995.

LET THE CUSTOMER DRIVE THE ORGANIZATION
(CHAPTER 3)

Albrecht, K., and Zemke, R. *Service America! Doing Business in the New Economy.* Chicago: Dow Jones Irwin, 1985.

Ashford, B. E., and R. H. Humphrey. "Emotional Labor in Service Roles: The Influence of Identity." *Academy of Management Review* (January 1993): 88–115.

Bell, C. R. *Customers as Partners: Building Relationships that Last.* San Francisco: Berrett-Koehler Publishers, 1994.

Bell, C. R., and Zemke, R. *Managing Knock Your Socks Off Service.* New York: AMACOM Books, 1992.

Brown, S. A. *Breakthrough Customer Service: Best Practices of Leaders in Customer Support.* Toronto, Ontario: John Wiley & Sons Canada, 1997.

Del Gaizo, E. R., K. J. Corcoran, and D. J. Erdman. *The Alligator Trap: How to Sell without Being Turned into a Pair of Shoes.* Chicago: Irwin, 1996.

Fishman, C. "How Can I Help You?" *Fast Company* (October/November 1997): 107–124.

Goleman, D. *Emotional Intelligence.* New York: Bantam Books, 1995.

Goleman, D. P. *Working with Emotional Intelligence.* New York: Bantam Books, 1998.

Heil G., T. Parker, and R. Tate. *Leadership and the Customer Revolution: The Messy, Unpredictable, and Inescapably Human Challenge of Making the Rhetoric of Change a Reality.* New York: John Wiley & Sons, 1994.

Heskett, J. L., W. E. Sasser, and L. A. Schlesinger. *The Service Profit Chain: How Leading Companies Link Profit and Growth to Loyalty, Satisfaction, and Value.* New York: Free Press, 1997.

Levesque, P. *The WOW Factory: Creating a Customer Focus Revolution in Your Business.* Chicago: Irwin, 1995.

McKenna, R. *Real Time: Preparing for the Age of the Never Satisfied Customer.* Cambridge, MA: Harvard Business School Press, 1997.

Reicheld, F. F., with T. Teal. *The Loyalty Effect: The Hidden Force Behind Growth, Profits, and Lasting Value.* Cambridge, MA: Harvard Business School Press, 1996.

Schaff, D. *Keeping the Service Edge: Giving Customers the Service They Demand.* New York: Dutton, 1995.

The Project on Disney. *Inside the Mouse: Work and Play at Disney World.* Durham, N.C.: Duke University Press, 1995.

INVOLVE EVERY MIND (CHAPTER 4)

Bellman, G. *Getting Things Done When You Are Not in Charge.* New York: Simon & Schuster, 1992.

Caminiti, S. "What Team Leaders Need to Know." *Fortune* (February 20, 1995): 93–100.

Cohen, S. G., and S. A. Mohrman. *Designing Team-Based Organizations: New Forms for Knowledge Work.* San Francisco: Jossey-Bass, 1995.

Frangos, S. J., and S. Bennett. *Team Zebra: How 1500 Partners Revitalized Eastman Kodak's Black and White Film-Making Flow.* Essex Junction, VT: Oliver Wright, 1993.

Guzzo, R. A., et al. *Team Effectiveness and Decision Making in Organizations.* San Francisco: Jossey-Bass, 1995.

Katz, A. J., D. Russ-Eft, L. Moran, and L. Ravishankar. "The Truth from the Trenches." In *The Handbook of Best Practices for Teams,* edited by G. M. Parker. Amherst, MA: HRD Press, 1996.

Kouzes, J., and Posner, B. *Encouraging the Heart: A Leader's Guide to Recognizing and Rewarding Others.* San Francisco: Jossey-Bass, 1999.

Lawler, E. *From the Ground Up.* San Francisco: Jossey-Bass, 1996.

Lawler, III, E. E. *The Ultimate Advantage: Creating the High-Involvement Organization.* San Francisco: Jossey-Bass, 1992.

Leonard, D., and S. Straus. "Putting Your Company's Whole Brain to Work." *Harvard Business Review* (July–August 1997): 110–121.

McLagan, P., and C. Nel. *The Age of Participation: New Governance for the Workplace and the World.* San Francisco: Berrett-Koehler, 1995.

Mohrman, S. A., S. G. Cohen, and A. M. Mohrman, Jr. *Designing Team-Based Organizations: New Forms for Knowledge Work.* San Francisco: Jossey-Bass, 1995.

Moran, L., E. Musselwhite, and J. H. Zenger. *Keeping Teams on Track.* Chicago: Irwin, 1996.

Orsburn, J. D., L. Moran, E. Musselwhite, and J. H. Zenger. *Self-Directed Work Teams: The American Challenge.* Homewood, IL: Business One Irwin, 1990.

Quinn, J. B., P. Anderson, and S. Finkelstein. "Managing Professional Intellect: Making the Most of the Best." *Harvard Business Review* (March–April 1996): 71–80.

Ray, D., and H. Bronstein. *Teaming Up.* New York: McGraw-Hill, 1995.

Robbins, H., and M. Finley. *Why Teams Don't Work: What Went Wrong and How to Make It Right.* Princeton, NJ: Perterson's/Pacesetter Books, 1995.

Smith, D. K. *Taking Charge of Change: 10 Principles for Managing People and Performance.* Reading, MA: Addison-Wesley, 1996.

Zenger, J. H., E. Musselwhite, K. Hurson, and C. Perrin. *Leading Teams.* Chicago: Irwin, 1994.

MANAGE WORK HORIZONTALLY (CHAPTER 5)

Ashkenas, R., D. Ulrich, T. Jick, and S. Kerr. *The Boundaryless Organization: Breaking the Chains of Organizational Structure.* San Francisco: Jossey-Bass, 1995.

Galbraith, J. R. *Designing Organizations: An Executive Briefing on Strategy, Structure, and Process.* San Francisco: Jossey-Bass, 1995.

Hamel, G., and C. K. Prahalad. *Competing for the Future.* Boston: Harvard Business School Press, 1994.

Hammer, M. *Beyond Reeningeering.* New York: HarperCollins, 1997.

Hammer, M., and J. Champy. *Reengineering the Corporation: A Manifesto for Business Revolution.* New York: Harper Business, 1993.

Hurson, K., J. Latham, and L. Moran. *Looking at Work Horizontally.* San Jose, CA: Zenger Miller, 1996.

Johann, B. *Designing Cross-Functional Business Processes.* San Francisco: Jossey-Bass, 1995.

Majchrzak, A., and Q. Wang. "Breaking the Functional Mind-Set in Process Organizations." *Harvard Business Review* (September–October 1996): 93–99.

Rummler, G. A., and A. P. Brache. *Improving Performance: How to Manage the White Space on the Organizational Chart.* San Francisco: Jossey-Bass, 1995.

BUILD PERSONAL CREDIBILITY (CHAPTER 6)

Block, P. *Stewardship: Choosing Service over Self-Interest.* San Francisco: Berrett-Koehler, 1993.

Conger, J. A., et al. *Spirit at Work: Discovering the Spirituality in Leadership.* San Francisco: Jossey-Bass, 1994.

Covey, S. R. *Principle-Centered Leadership.* New York: Simon & Schuster, 1990.

Goleman, D. *Emotional Intelligence: Why It Can Matter More than IQ.* New York: Bantam Books, 1995.

Kouzes, J. M., and B. Z. Posner. *Credibility.* San Francisco: Jossey-Bass, 1993.

OTHER READINGS

Bennis, W. G. *On Becoming a Leader.* Reading, MA: Addison-Wesley, 1989.

Bennis, W. G. "The Leader as Storyteller." *Harvard Business Review* (January–February 1996): 2–4, 6.

Bennis, W. G., and B. Nanus. *Leaders: The Strategies for Taking Charge.* New York: Harper & Row, 1985.

Collins, D. R., and J. I. Porras. *Built to Last: Successful Habits of Visionary Companies.* New York: Harper Collins, 1994.

Drucker, P. *Managing in a Time of Great Change.* New York: Dutton-Truman Talley Books, 1995.

Gardner, H. *Leading Minds: An Anatomy of Leadership.* New York: Basic Books, 1995.

Gardner, J. W. *On Leadership.* New York: Free Press, 1990.

Hesselbein, F., M. Goldsmith, and R. Beckhard, editors. *The Leader of the Future.* San Francisco: Jossey-Bass, 1996.

Katzenbach, J. R. *Real Change Leaders: How You Create Growth and High Performance at Your Company.* New York: McKinsey & Company, 1995.

Kotter, J. P. *The Leadership Factor.* New York: Free Press, 1988.

Kouzes, J. M. and B. Z. Posner. *The Leadership Challenge: How to Get Extraordinary Things Done in Organizations.* Revised. San Francisco: Jossey-Bass, 1995.

Tichy, N., with E. Cohen. *The Leadership Engine: How Winning Companies Build Leaders at Every Level.* New York: Harper Collins, 1997.

Tichy, N., and M. A. Devanna. *The Transformational Leader.* New York: Wiley, 1986.

Wheatley, M. *Leadership and the New Science: Learning About Organization From an Orderly Universe, 1st Edition.* San Francisco: Berrett-Koehler Publishers, 1992.

REFERENCES

Bretz, R. D., and R. E. Thompsett. "Comparing Traditional and Integrative Learning Methods in Organizational Training Programs." *Journal of Applied Psychology,* 77, no. 6 (1992): pp. 941-951.

Dixon, N. "The Relationship between Trainee Responses on Participant Reaction Forms and Posttest Scores." *Human Resource Development Quarterly,* 1, no. 2 (1990): pp. 129-138.

Flanagan, J. C. "The Critical Incident Technique." *Psychological Bulletin,* 51, no. 4 (1954): pp. 327-358.

Kirkpatrick, D. L. "Techniques for Evaluating Programs." *Journal of the American Society of Training Directors (Training & Development),* 13, no. 11 (1959a): pp. 3-9.

Kirkpatrick, D. L. "Techniques for Evaluating Programs: Part 2: Learning." *Journal of the American Society of Training Directors (Training & Development),* 13, no. 12 (1959b): pp. 21-26.

Kirkpatrick, D. L. "Techniques for Evaluating Programs: Part 3: Behavior." *Journal of the American Society of Training Directors (Training & Development),* 14, no. 1 (1960a): pp. 13-18.

Kirkpatrick, D. L. "Techniques for Evaluating Programs: Part 4: Results." *Journal of the American Society of Training Directors (Training & Development),* 14, no. 1 (1960b): pp. 28-32.

Kirkpatrick, D. L. *Evaluating training programs: The four levels.* San Francisco: Berrett-Koehler, 1994.

Russ-Eft, D. "Defining Competencies: A Critique." *Human Resource Development Quarterly,* 6, no. 4 (1995): pp. 329-335.

INDEX

ABOUT THE AUTHORS

Horst A. Bergmann   is a senior business executive with more than 35 years of broad international leadership experience. By focusing on the requirements and challenges faced by people at every level of an organization, he has created global businesses with remarkable records of revenue and profit growth. Mr. Bergmann currently holds three top leadership positions: President and Chief Executive Officer of AchieveGlobal, an international provider of performance skills training and consulting; President and Chief Executive Officer of Jeppesen Sanderson, an international aviation information company; and Executive Vice President of Times Mirror, the parent company of both AchieveGlobal and Jeppesen Sanderson, and of a number of leading newspapers, including the *Los Angeles Times*.

Kathleen Hurson   is Vice President of Research and Development for AchieveGlobal. She is a principal author of three award-winning AchieveGlobal leadership training programs: FrontLine Leadership, TeamLeadership, and Leadership 2000. These programs have been translated into 14 languages and are used by thousands of organizations around the world. Ms. Hurson is a frequent speaker on leadership at such groups as the American Society for Training and Development, the American Society for Quality Control, and annual meetings of Human Resource Executive. Her recent publications include the book, "Leading Teams: Mastering the New Role," and "Why Doesn't This Team Work? A Case Commentary," which appeared in the *Harvard Business Review*.

Darlene Russ-Eft, Ph.D., is Director of Research Services at AchieveGlobal. Dr. Russ-Eft received the 1996 Editor of the Year Award from Times Mirror for her research work, and is currently Associate Editor of *Human Resource Development Quarterly*. She is Past Chair of the Research Committee of the American Society for Training and Development (ASTD), a member of the Research Committee of the Instructional Systems Association, and a member of the Board of the American Evaluation Association. Dr. Russ-Eft has published over 50 research articles, as well as four books on training and development and adult education research. She is a frequent speaker at conferences world-wide.

ABOUT ACHIEVEGLOBAL

AchieveGlobal, Inc., a division of the Times Mirror Company, is the world's largest provider of performance skills training and consulting. It represents the integration of three leaders in their respective fields: Kaset International in customer loyalty, Learning International in sales performance, and Zenger Miller in leadership and organizational effectiveness.

With nearly 1,000 employees in 44 offices across North America, affiliate partners in more than 40 countries, and training in over 40 languages and dialects, AchieveGlobal serves more than 400 of the Fortune 500 companies and more than 300 of the Canadian Financial Post 500 companies. You can learn more about AchieveGlobal and its products and services on their web site at www.achieveglobal.com or by calling 1-800-456-9390.